CONFUCIANISM AND ITS RIVALS

BY

HERBERT A. GILES, LL.D.

First published in 1915

Published by Left of Brain Books

Copyright © 2023 Left of Brain Books

ISBN 978-1-396-32308-9

First Edition

All rights reserved. No part of this publication may be reproduced, distributed, or transmitted in any form or by any means, including photocopying, recording, or other electronic or mechanical methods, without the prior written permission of the publisher, except in the case of brief quotations permitted by copyright law. Left of Brain Books is a division of Left Of Brain Onboarding Pty Ltd.

PUBLISHER'S PREFACE

About the Book

"China is home to two major world religions, Confiucianism and Taoism, and also played an important role in the historical development of a third, Northern Buddhism. Eventually, Confucianism became the state religion, and, purged of metaphysical aspects, the dominant Chinese religion until the 20th century. Other religions, including Christianity, Judaism, and Islam, have all had indigenous expressions as well.

Giles covers the entire history of Chinese religion in this book, which was originally delivered as one of the Hibbert lectures in 1914. Herbert Allen Giles (b. Dec. 8, 1845, d. Feb. 13, 1935), was a British diplomat and an old China hand. He is best known for his role in developing the Wade-Giles system of transliterating Chinese. Giles was the father of Lionel Giles, who was also a distinguished orientalist, and translator of Sun Tzu's Art of War, among others."

(Quote from sacred-texts.com)

About the Author

Giles, Herbert Allen (1845 - 1935)

"Herbert Allen Giles (8 December 1845 - 13 February 1935) was a British diplomat and sinologist, educated at Charterhouse.

Giles was a diplomat to China (1867-1892). He was British Vice Consul at Pagoda Island (1880-83) and Shanghai (1883-85) and Consul at Tamsui (1885-91) and at Ningpo (1891-93) who later became the second professor of Chinese at Cambridge, succeeding Wade, after living in Aberdeen, Scotland. In 1902 he became first lecturer at Columbia University on the Lung Foundation."

(Quote from wikipedia.org)

CONTENTS

PUBLISHER'S PREFACE
PREFACE 1
   B.C. 3000-1200 2
   B.C. 1200-500 23
   B.C. 500-300 44
   B.C. 300-200 63
   B.C. 200-A.D. 100 84
   A.D. 100-600 105
   A.D. 600-1000 123
   A.D. 1000-1915 142

PREFACE

IN the following Lectures an attempt is made to exhibit chronologically, the principles and practice adopted by Confucius as a heritage from antiquity and subsequently handed down through twenty-four centuries, with certain modifications, until the present day.

Beginning from the pure monotheism of a personal God, we ultimately reach the substitution of Confucius and of his worship, with the almost total disappearance of a supernatural Power. This development was not effected with the consent of all parties concerned. Taoism, Buddhism, Mazdaism, Judaism, Mahometanism, and Christianity under such varied forms as Manichæism, Nestorianism, Roman Catholicism, and Protestantism, each made its bid for the salvation of the Chinese, with results which it is hoped may be gathered from this volume.

My best thanks are due to the Hibbert Trustees for allowing me an opportunity of drawing attention, from a purely secular point of view, to the religious struggles and problems of a people whose national life dates back to prehistoric times and still shows no signs of decay.

HERBERT A. GILES.

CAMBRIDGE, 1st May, 1915.

B.C. 3000-1200

THE Chinese are not, and, so far as we can judge from their history, never have been, what we understand by the term "a religious people." Consequently, we find in their biographical records extraordinarily few instances of religious fanaticism, bigotry, and persecu-tion; still fewer, if any, examples of men and women who have suffered for their faith, when mere verbal recantation would have saved them from a dreaded fate. With a highly practical nation like the Chinese, the acts of human beings have always been reckoned as of infinitely greater importance than their opinions. The value of morality has completely oversha-dowed any claims of belief; duty towards one's neighbour has mostly taken precedence of duty towards God.

The word "God" has been familiar in China from time immemorial; but before we can deal with the conception implied thereby, it will be necessary to turn our attention to the visible universe as it appeared to the primeval Chinese man. Above him was a round sky, later on to be symbolized as the male element in creation; below him was a square earth, also to be symbolized later on as the mother of all things—the *feme covert* in "the bridal of the earth and sky."

In the Canon of Changes, usually admitted to be the oldest extant Chinese book, we read: "The sky one, the earth two, the sky three, the earth four, the sky five, the earth six, the sky seven, the earth eight, the sky nine, the earth ten." This is explained to mean that, in a cosmogonical sense, and also for purposes of divination, odd numbers are male, even numbers female.

We must pause a moment to consider what the Canon of Changes precisely is. Broadly speaking, it is the most venerated as well as the most ancient volume of a collection of sacred books now known as the Confucian Canon, and it is said to have come into existence as follows. Three thousand years before Christ—the furthest point reached even by the most enthusiastic chronologers—China was ruled by her first, somewhat legendary monarch, the Emperor Fu Hsi. Prior to this date, we hear of a Chinese Prometheus, the discoverer of fire, and of a still earlier hero, who taught mankind to make nest-habitations in trees, as a safeguard against such attacks from animals as people would be more exposed to on the ground.

The Emperor Fu Hsi is said to have been miraculously conceived by his mother, and to have been born after a gestation of twelve years; but in spite of this, and of other legendary accretions, it is most probable that he had a real existence. He taught his people to hunt, to fish, and to keep flocks. He showed them how to split the wood of a certain tree (*Pawlonia imperialis*, S. and Z.), and then how to twist threads and stretch them across so as to form rude musical instruments. He invented some kind of calendar, placed the marriage-contract upon a proper basis, and introduced cooked as opposed to raw food. From certain markings, divinely revealed to him on the back of a tortoise—some say a dragon (hence the Imperial Dragon)—he is said to have constructed the Eight Diagrams, or series of lines from which was to be ultimately developed a scheme of divination, as embodied many centuries later in the Canon of Changes.

Put in the fewest words, these Diagrams are the eight possible combinations or arrangements of a line and a broken line in groups of three, so that either one or the other is repeated twice, and in two cases three times, in the same combination. Thus, there may be a broken line above or below two unbroken lines, two broken lines above or below one unbroken line, a broken line between two unbroken lines, an unbroken line between two

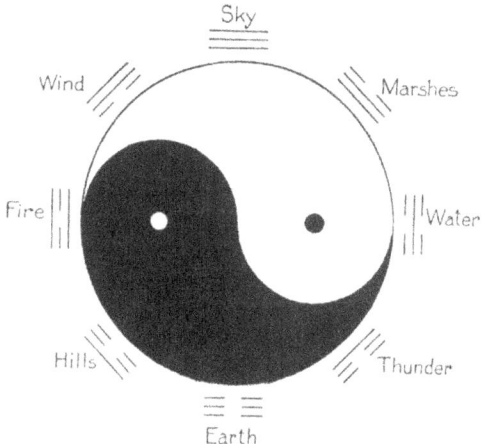

broken lines, and finally, a diagram of three unbroken lines, and another of three broken lines. Of these last two, the former, three unbroken lines, was held to represent the sky; the latter, three broken lines, stood for the earth. The remaining six figures were identified as symbols of mist, fire, thunder, wind, water, and hills; and on the ground that the sky and earth, the male and female principles in nature, produce, as it were, the other six elements, an attempt has been made to trace a connexion between the Eight Diagrams and the company assembled in the Ark.

The Emperor Fu Hsi is said by some to have subsequently increased these combinations, as above, to sixty-four, by the simple process of doubling the number of lines employed; and on this groundwork was first of all constructed, according to tradition—for no definite traces remain in literature—a system of divination, of which we know next to nothing. However, in the twelfth century B.C., King Wên, the virtual founder of the great Chow dynasty, called "King" although he never really occupied the throne, was cast into prison for sedition by the reigning tyrant, whom King Wên's son afterwards overthrew. There he passed two years, occupying himself with the Diagrams, which others say he, and not the Emperor Fu Hsi, increased to sixty-four, finally producing sixty-four short essays, enigmatically and symbolically expressed, on important themes, mostly of a moral, social, or political character. This text is followed by certain commentaries, called by the Chinese the "Ten Wings," admittedly of a later date, and usually attributed, but without foundation, to Confucius, who has left it on record that had a number of years been added to his life, he would have devoted fifty of them to a further study of the Canon of Changes, and could then have claimed to be without great faults. It is indeed recorded by China's most famous historian, Ssŭ-ma Ch'ien (d. *circa* B.C. 80), that Confucius perused and reperused this work so often that the leather strings on which the wooden tablets in use at that date were strung, gave way, first and last, three times, from sheer wear and tear.

The foreign student is disappointed when he comes to a study of the Canon of Changes; partly because of the exaggerated value set upon its contents by native scholars of all ages, and partly from an inability to penetrate its labyrinthine mysteries and seize the hidden spirit of the book. It has been alleged by Chinese enthusiasts that, if you have only the wit to seek, you will find in the Canon of Changes the germs of all the great scientific discoveries; on the other hand, it was reserved for two foreign students (Sir R. Douglas and Terrien de Lacouperie) to put their heads together and publicly announce that this work, regarded in China as based on a divine revelation, is nothing more than a vocabulary of an obscure Central Asian tribe—so obscure indeed that to this day it remains unlocated and unknown.

A translation of the Canon of Changes was made by Dr Legge, the greatest Chinese scholar of modern times at the day of his death. Dr Legge thought that he had "found the key," but it is doubtful if anyone else has ever shared with him that opinion. Let us take the first Diagram, which originally consisted of three horizontal lines, afterwards doubled, and supposed to represent the sky. King Wên tells us that the whole Diagram symbolizes "what is great and originating, penetrating, advantageous, correct, and firm." King Wên's fourth son, the Duke of Chow, one of China's best-loved figures in history, added, or is said to have added, an analysis of the Diagram, taking it line by line. Thus, in the first line he discovers a dragon lying hidden in the abyss; upon which he declares that "it is not time for active doing." In the second line we have the dragon again, but in this case "appearing in the open." "It will be advantageous," says the Duke, "to meet with a great man." And so on—for those who can understand how one straight line can yield a certain meaning, and another similar straight line another and quite a different meaning. Take a still further exasperating specimen of what we read in this relic of antiquity, on which more numerous and more voluminous commentaries have been written than on the Old and New Testaments combined.

Text.—The first line, divided, shows a man moving his great toes.

Wing.—He moves his great toes;—his mind is set on what is beyond himself.

Text.—The fifth line, undivided, shows a man moving the flesh along the spine, above the heart. There will be no occasion for repentance.

Wing.—He moves the flesh along the spine, above the heart;—his aim is trivial.

Just on eight hundred years after the revelation of the Eight Diagrams to the Emperor Fu Hsi, came another revelation, which was subsequently recognized as complementary of the first, and is now closely associated with it in the philosophical speculations of the scholars of the Sung dynasty, who flourished some seven to eight hundred years ago, and will be referred to later on. In B.C. 2205 the Great Yü, as he was afterwards called, ascended the throne of China. His birth, like that of most of China's heroes, had been miraculous; and it is recorded that four days after his marriage he started forth to drain the empire of the waters of a disastrous flood, which some have tried to identify with the Noachian Deluge. Another divinely sent tortoise appears to have risen from the waters and to have presented him—some say the recipient was really the Emperor Fu Hsi of old—with a numerical scheme, or arrangement of groups of the cardinal numbers 1 to 9, known as the River Plan, by means of which divination was raised to the position of a science, as it is found at the present day.

The final arrangement of the River Plan, after many modifications, was as follows:—

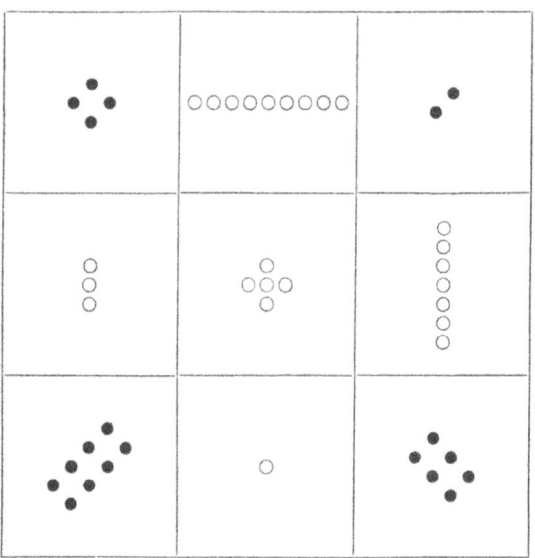

These groups, added up vertically, horizontally, or diagonally, always yield a total of fifteen.

Other methods were employed, especially one, as we shall see by and by, in which a certain magic grass, or reed, played the chief part; but it is now time, after this long digression, to return to the sky and earth.

At a very remote period, long before the Canon of Changes had received its first impress from the hands of King Wên, the Chinese people had already come to regard the sky as the home or habitat of a powerful Being who took a marked interest in human affairs. This Being may have been suggested, according to Buckle's theory, by lightning, thunder, earthquakes, the revolutions of the sun and moon, and similar phenomena. The name given to the Being—it is still in use—was *T'ien*, a word which, for reasons to be presently brought forward, we are unable to render adequately by any other term than "God." The first of these reasons is that so soon as the Chinese began to express thought through the medium of a script, the symbol set down for *T'ien* was a rude picture, such as a child or savage might draw, of a human being: 大. This anthropomorphic character occurs in inscriptions on sacrificial cauldrons which date back to B.C. 1100, when the written language had already become a vehicle of considerable precision. It is often found, for instance, in conjunction with the word "son," meaning "Son of God," a title which has always been applied to the Emperors of China, but which association and convention compel us to render by the less startling "Son of Heaven." Translators of Chinese texts have indeed generally tried to shirk the use of the word God " as an equivalent for *T'ien*, and have adopted the vaguer word "Heaven"; against which it may be urged that this latter term rather tends to obscure the idea of a personal Deity, and is better reserved for the celestial habitation of God and of spirits, in which sense, together with that of "sky," the word *t'ien* came also to be used.

Later inscriptions show the character *T'ien* in process of modification, 天, towards the modern sign in use at the present day. The head is flattened to a straight line, but the remainder is still suggestive of a body with arms and legs. To-day we write 天, a character which has been accepted by native scholars, who had failed to pick up the real clue, as a combination of — *one*, and 大 *great*—the one great thing. [1]

Such, indeed, is the etymological analysis given in the *Shuo Wên*, a dictionary which was produced about one hundred years after the Christian era, and has been the recognized authority ever since. Whether by "the one great thing" the author may have meant the sky only, or heaven as

---

[1] This development was first pointed out by Mr L. C. Hopkins, I.S.O.

used by us in two senses, namely, the sky and God, it is impossible to say for certain; the analysis, which ignores altogether the picture element, certainly points in the direction of the former view. There is, in fact, little doubt that even before the date of the Christian era the idea of an anthropomorphic God had somewhat weakened in its hold upon the Chinese mind, and that the word *T'ien* had become more closely associated with the material heavens, the sky. Thus, the philosopher Hsün Tzŭ, of the third century B.C., says, "*T'ien* has no concrete form; all the void expanse above the earth is *t'ien*." Here, of course, he is speaking only of Lien, the sky; in a future lecture we shall see what he has to say about *T'ien*, God. It is rather to the older works of the Confucian Canon that we must turn for the ancient Chinese belief in an anthropomorphic, and therefore personal, God. In the so-called Canon of History, which is a collection of miscellaneous documents of an historical character, extending over a period from the twenty-fourth to the eighth century B.C., and said to have been edited under its present form by Confucius himself, we find the word *T'ien* largely used in the sense of "God," and very sparsely used in the sense of "sky."

There is a single instance of the word *T'ien* used in the restricted sense of heaven, the abode of the Deity. It occurs in a prayer, patriotically offered up, in B.C. 1120, to the immediate canonized ancestors of the first king of the Chow dynasty, who was dangerously ill, and runs as follows: "If you three kings have charge in *t'ien*, heaven, of your great descendant, let my life be a substitute for his."

Almost, however, at the beginning of the Canon of History, and before there is any mention of *T'ien*, we are faced by another term which has been widely adopted by Christian missionaries, under the skilled leadership of Dr Legge, as the one and only correct equivalent for "God." This is *Shang Ti*, meaning Supreme Ruler. I freely confess that for many years I regarded Dr Legge's position as unassailable, and I am still on his side as regards the impropriety of another term, *Shin* or *Shên*, "spirit," which found favour chiefly with American missionaries under the guidance of distinguished colleagues, among whom was also the British missionary and lexicographer, Dr Morrison. The view of Dr Morrison need not be seriously considered, based as it was, by his own admission, upon a desire to convince the Chinese that "their ideas of *Shin* were erroneous."

A longer and closer acquaintance with the Confucian Canon has satisfied me that the proper equivalent of our word "God" is *T'ien*; and that *Shang*

Ti, "Supreme Ruler," was originally a mere epithet of *T'ien*, but gradually came to be employed almost in the sense of another Being, yet not another Being; thus forming, as I hope to show in my next lecture, a Godhead of two Persons. It is perhaps but a minor advantage that to express in Chinese our own monosyllabic term, we need use no more than a single word; but we cannot overlook the fact that *T'ien* was the very term suggested by the learned Manchu Emperor, K'ang Hsi, as a settlement of the question in the seventeenth century. But I am anticipating, and 1 will now return to the Canon of History.

Here we find that *T'ien* is used in the sense of "God" more than one hundred and fifty times, whereas *Shang Ti* occurs only about twenty times; and, in the words of Dr Legge, this "supreme, governing Power is understood to be omniscient, omnipotent, and righteous." To these characteristics, notwithstanding the anthropomorphism of which I have already spoken, it will be necessary to add that of omnipresence, unless it be conceded that from a given point in the universe God can practically see and hear all men—which amounts to the same thing. Old proverbial literature, still of everyday application, tells us that "the whispers of men sound like thunder to God," that "the eye of God sees clearly, and rewards promptly," that "you may deceive man, but not God," with many other sayings of similar import. All these are formed with the word *T'ien*; there is not a single saying of the kind, known to me, which is based upon the use of *Shang Ti*.

A few examples from the Canon of History may be noted, to enable us to form an idea of the Deity as conceived of in China twenty centuries or so before the Christian era. In a brief account of the Great Yü and his engineering labours, one of his ministers says to him, "O Emperor, Almighty God regarded you with favour, so that the Four Seas became yours, and you yourself the lord of all beneath the canopy of heaven." This passage contains *T'ien* under both of its received senses, God and the sky; it further illustrates the relation which, up to two years ago, had always been felt to exist between the Emperor and his people. To realize this latter point to the full, we may be allowed once more to anticipate and turn to the works of Mencius, fourth and third centuries B.C., where allusion is made to the ancient Emperors, Yao and Shun, the immediate predecessors of the Great Yü, the former of whom, Yao, abdicated in favour of Shun, a virtuous peasant. "Did Yao really give the empire to Shun?" asked a disciple. Mencius said, "No. The Emperor (literally the Son of God) cannot give the empire to another." "Yes," replied the disciple, "but Shun got it. Who gave it to him?" "God gave it to him," was the answer. "When God gave it," pursued the disciple, "did He explain to Shun what his duties would be?" Mencius said, "No. God does not speak. God made manifest His will through Shun's own behaviour." "How was this effected?" asked the disciple. "The Emperor," replied Mencius, "can present a man to God, but he cannot make God give that man the empire. Yao presented Shun to God, and God accepted him; he exhibited Shun to the people, and the people accepted him." To the disciple, who pleaded for further enlightenment, Mencius said, "Yao caused Shun to preside over the sacrifices, and the spirits were well pleased; therefore God accepted him. Yao also caused him to preside over the conduct of affairs, and affairs were well administered and a general well-being prevailed; therefore the people accepted him. Thus, it was God and the people who gave Shun the empire; an Emperor cannot give the empire to another."

Let us take one more passage from the Canon of History, which deals with a period at the close of the eighteenth century B.C. The Hsia dynasty, founded by the Great Yü in 2205, had passed away amid scenes of rebellion and bloodshed; such scenes indeed as have since been witnessed at the fall of every dynasty which, by corruption and misrule, has forfeited the mandate and protection of God. The last ruler of this house had for many years indulged in cruel brutality and lust almost unparalleled in history. His utter wickedness was even said to have caused two rivers to dry up, so prone were the Chinese always to attribute unpropitious natural phenomena to manifestations of divine displeasure with the occupant of the throne. To one of his ministers who remonstrated with him, he replied, "I am to the empire what the sun is to the sky; when the sun goes, I shall." He then caused the minister to be put to death. Thereupon the prince of Shang, a virtuous hero, took up arms against him. The Imperial forces were overwhelmed, and the Emperor was sent into banishment, where three years later he died. His son fled northwards, and is said to have founded the tribe of Hun-yü, which we are now able to identify with the Huns. The prince of Shang, known in history as Ch'êng T'ang, or T'ang the Completer, was raised to the throne, and led a blameless life; but his successor, a grandson, fell away from virtue, and incurred the respectful remonstrances of his grandfather's trusted minister, as follows: "His late Majesty kept his eye fixed upon the clear commands of God, reverently serving the spirits of heaven and the lower world, of the land and grain, and of deceased ancestors. God took note of his virtuous conduct, and conferred upon him the great office, that he might give peace to all parts of the empire." Again, the same minister said, "Ah! God has no partialities; only to those who are reverent does He show favour. The people are not constant in their affections, except to those (rulers) who have charity of heart. The spirits do not necessarily enjoy sacrifices; what they enjoy is the sincerity." And then he urges the new ruler to emulate the virtues of his grandfather, who, he declared, had become "fit to take his place by God."

We are not here interested in the historical fact that the above remonstrances were successful; our object in bringing forward these quotations is to establish the theory, if possible, beyond question, that the ancient Chinese believed in an anthropomorphic, personal God, whose dwelling was in the heavens above. Incidentally, we have to consider allusions to spirits and to sacrifices, both of which will be found to have an important bearing on the subject.

So far back as twenty-two centuries and more before the birth of Christ, we have a record of the Emperor Shun sacrificing, not only with a burnt offering to God, but also to the spirits of hills and rivers, and under a collective term to spirits in general. Later, we find the Great Yü sacrificing to certain mountains, Ch'êng T'ang taking into account the colour of a victim, and sacrifices offered to the spirit of a deceased ruler. Warnings are given that there should be moderation even in these solemn religious exercises; and one monarch is advised to devote less attention to the spirit of his father and more to the spirits of his predecessors on the throne. The use of incense, which has been dated by some writers from the introduction of Buddhism, appears to have been practised by the Chinese in the very earliest ages, and the fat for the burnt offering has been shown to survive in the candles still to be seen in the ceremonies of the Confucian temple. Worship seems to have been mostly associated with buildings, though open-air altars were not uncommon; as, for instance, in the case we have already dealt with, of prayer offered up for a sick king, when three altars were set up for that purpose. "Temple" is perhaps too majestic a term for remote antiquity; what is intended may be often better expressed by some such word as "shrine." As to the worship of ancestors, on which great stress is laid in these early records, I may point out, not for the first, though I trust it will be for the last time, that those who compare the offerings of meat and wine by Confucian mourners with the tribute of flowers placed upon graves by Christian mourners, "do greatly err." Ancestral worship, deeply ingrained as it is in the Chinese mind, is one of the great obstacles to the Christianization of China; and many worthy and well-meaning missionaries, going so far back even as the Jesuits of the seventeenth century, have pleaded for the admission of this apparently harmless rite among the devotional duties of the Christian convert. Other missionaries, however, have set their faces against such a concession, correctly feeling that the main object of ancestral worship in China is to secure from the spirits of dead ancestors, in return for offerings of food and fruit at graves, protection and advancement of worldly interests, which would be incompatible with the teachings of Christianity.

The "Do ut des" principle does not lift prayer to a very elevated plane, but it must be admitted that this principle looms large in the sacrifices which the Chinese have been in the habit of offering to the Deity, as well as to their deceased ancestors. There is a story, which properly belongs to the fourth century B.C., that when one of the feudal States was about to attack another State, the ruling prince of the latter instructed his son-in-law, whose nickname was Grease-pot, because of his oily tongue, to proceed to a third State and ask for military assistance, taking with him one hundred pounds' weight of silver and ten chariots as a bribe to that end. On hearing this order, the son-in-law laughed so immoderately that he snapped the lash which fastened his cap under his chin; and when the prince asked him to explain, he said, "As I was coming along this morning, I saw a husbandman offering up in sacrifice a pig's foot and a small cup of wine; after which he prayed, saying, O God, make my upper terraces fill baskets, and my lower terraces fill carts; make my fields bloom with crops, and my barns burst with grain! And I could not help laughing at the thought of a man who offered so little and wanted so much." The prince took the hint, and obtained the assistance required.

We shall have occasion again to deal with both prayer and sacrifice; and we will now leave the Canon of History and proceed to an examination of the Canon of Poetry, the next in order among the sacred books of Confucianism. It may here be mentioned that the term "Confucianism" must be taken to cover the old moral and religious teachings of pre-Confucian as well as of post-Confucian days. In a well-worn sentence, Confucius expressly disclaimed any credit for his work, declaring that he was merely handing on those lessons of antiquity which he believed in and loved so well.

The scope of the Canon of Poetry may be described in a few words. In addition to the literary labours already mentioned, and others to which we shall come in due course, Confucius, clearly recognizing that if he could have a hand in merely editing the people's ballads, anyone might make their laws, set himself to the task of examining his country's poetry with that special object in view. It seems that at his date, roughly five hundred years before Christ, there existed a collection of some three thousand ancient pieces. Of these, Confucius selected three hundred and eleven, of six of which only the titles remained, rejecting many of the others as being mere repetitions, and many more as containing, in modern parlance, "words and expressions which cannot with propriety be read aloud in a family," thus anticipating Dr Bowdler by something like twenty-two centuries. Whatever people may think of Dr Bowdler and his belated efforts to expurgate Shakespeare, China certainly owes a deep debt to Confucius for having initiated a decency of thought and expression which has placed Chinese literature, in that respect if in no other, above every literature in the world.

These three hundred and five "Odes," to use the title under which they are popularly known, are, like all Chinese poetry, in rhyme, and were originally sung to music and accompanied by dancing. They are subdivided under three heads, namely, National Ballads, Lamentations and Panegyrics, and Sacrificial Poems. There is a great deal more to be said about this wonderful collection of old-world Odes, but we are concerned at the moment rather with what we may find in them germane to our present subject.

As may well be imagined, the National Ballads, the first of the three subdivisions, do not yield much to the searcher after traces of religious thought. These deal chiefly with love, marriage, and the chase. Only on rare occasions is there a sudden appeal to the Deity—in all cases *T'ien*; usually nothing more than "O God!"; in two or three instances, "O Thou distant God in the blue!" reminding one of the Indian ryot's cry, "God is great, but He is too far off."

From the Panegyrics we may glean several more definite allusions. There is one ode which was evidently sung at a banquet given by the king, and addressed to the king. The first three verses each begin:

> God protects and establishes thee,

and one verse continues:

> So that in everything thou dost prosper.

The most important lines are:

> With happy auspices and purifications thou bringest the sacrifices,
> And dost filially present them,
> In spring, summer, autumn, and winter,
> To former rulers,
> Who say, We give to thee
> Myriads of years of life unending.
> Their spirits come
> And confer on thee many blessings.

Hereafter we light frequently upon the favourite term for "Emperor," always to be rendered Son of Heaven, it being awkward for us, as already stated, to translate by "Son of God." There is a further reason for not adopting this latter nomenclature, namely, that the Emperor has been uniformly regarded as the son of God by adoption only, and liable to be displaced from that position as a punishment for the offence of misrule. There is no pretence of any such relationship between Father and Son as is recognized by orthodox Christians. So long as the ruler was accepted by God and the people, he may be said to have occupied the throne by divine right, and by common consent was hedged in by the same divinity as that accorded to kings in western nations. But if the ruler failed in his duties, the obligation of the people was at an end, and his divine right disappeared simultaneously. Of this we have an example in a portion of the Canon to be examined by and by. Under the year 558 B.C. we find the following narrative. One of the feudal princes asked an official, saying, "Have not the people of the Wei State done very wrong in expelling their ruler?" "Perhaps the ruler himself," was the reply, "may have done very wrong. A good ruler will reward the virtuous and punish the vicious; he will nourish his people as his children, covering them as the sky and supporting them as the earth. Then the people will honour the ruler, love him as a parent, look up to him as the sun and moon, revere him as they do spiritual beings, and stand in awe of him as of thunder. But if the life of the people is impoverished, and if the spirits are deprived of their sacrifices, of what use is the ruler, and what can the people do but get rid of him?"

In one of the Lamentations we find the Deity charged with want of pity and with injustice:

> Almighty God, unjust,
> Is sending down these exhausting disorders;
> Almighty God, unkind,
> Is sending down these great miseries.
> O Almighty God, without pity,
> There is no end to the disorder!

The next passage I shall quote contains within the space of six lines both terms for God, *T'ien* and *Shang Ti*, in the order just given. The translation may be varied thus:

> The people, now amid their perils,
> Look up to *T'ien*, God, who is inscrutable;
> But if His determination has once been fixed,
> There is no one whom He will not overcome.
> This mighty *Shang Ti*, Supreme Ruler,
> Does He hate anyone?

As another instance of the familiar way in which protests are addressed to the Deity, we have:

> O great God Almighty,
> Why has Thy mercy been withheld?
> Why send down death and famine,
> Destroying all throughout the kingdom?

With one more example we will leave the Lamentations:

> O Thou far-off, Almighty God,
> Who art called our Father and Mother!

We now revert to the Panegyrics, the first of which is in honour of King Wên, the real founder, as before stated, of the Chow dynasty, in 1122 B.C.

> King Wên is up on high,
> Sharing in the glory of God.
> Although Chow was an old country,
> Its mandate has but just come.
> Was not Chow illustrious?
> And was not the ruler's mandate opportune?

> King Wên now ascends and descends,
> Moving about the person of God.

Here, in the first case, the Chinese word for God is *T'ien*; in the second case, it is *Ti*, Ruler, the latter half of *Shang Ti*, Supreme Ruler. Another verse, in which *Shang Ti* is employed, runs thus:

> Ever think of your forefather (King Wên),
> Cultivating your virtue,
> Striving to do the will of God;
> So shall you obtain much happiness.
> Before the late rulers lost their following,
> They could sit alongside of *Shang Ti*, God;
> Look on them as you look on a mirror,
> For God's will is not easily carried out.

The next verse contains two singular lines:

> The doings of Almighty God (here *T'ien*)
> Have neither sound nor smell;

meaning, of course, that His ways are inscrutable to man, who is dependent upon the faculties of physical perception.

The next panegyric is noteworthy, not only for itself, but because its first verse was completely misunderstood by Dr Legge, who, like Homer, sometimes, but very rarely, nods. It refers, as indeed do all the first eight panegyrics of this section, to King Wên, the remaining two celebrating the glories of his great warrior son, King Wu. If my new rendering proves to be intelligible, that will be a great point gained; for intelligibility is, *cæteris paribus*, the touchstone of correct translation from the Chinese.

> A man must show himself brightly virtuous on earth,
> Then comes the exercise of majestic power from above.
> God has difficulty in trusting anyone,
> For it is not easy to be a king;
> The rightful heir of the last dynasty
> Was not permitted to possess the kingdom

Instead of

> God has difficulty in trusting anyone,

Dr Legge has

> Heaven is not readily to be relied upon,

which is quite out of keeping with the context, though abuse of God—Dr Legge generally tried to avoid the ineffable Name—is quite in keeping, as will be seen further on, with the ordinary Chinese attitude towards the Deity. This ode goes on to describe King Wên's birth, and then his marriage.

> God chose for him a mate,
> A lady from a powerful kingdom,
> Like unto a younger sister of God Himself.

Then comes the birth of his son, King Wu, followed by the rebellion in which both father and son took part; and finally, the great battle in which, thirteen years after his father's death, King Wu overthrew the reigning dynasty, and mounted the throne as first suzerain under the feudal system of the House of Chow. "God is on your side," was the cry which rang in King Wu's ears; "have no doubts in your heart!"

There seems to have been an early chieftain of these Chow people, before their rise to power, who taught his tribesmen to make cave-dwellings and kiln-shaped huts; and who afterwards led them on the great trek by which they reached the beautiful and rich plain whereon, as the panegyric tells us, grew violets and the edible sowthistle in abundance. It was apparently an ideal spot; but before deciding to make it his final resting-place, the leader of the host had recourse, as usual, to divination.

> He singed (some say "pierced") the tortoise-shell,
> And the response was to stay;
> Whereupon they set to building houses.

We do not know for certain the process by which the omens were obtained from the tortoise-shell,[1] or from grain, which was also used for this

---

[1] See *La Divination par l'Ecaille de Tortue*, by Professor E. Chavannes (*Journal Asiatique*, Janvier-Février, 1911).

purpose; it is easier perhaps to understand the use of the reeds. In a case of a young man suggesting elopement to a girl, the latter replies,

> You say that you have consulted the tortoise-shell and the reeds,
> And that there is nothing unfavourable in their responses;
> Therefore come, with your carriage,
> And I will pack up and go with you.

The tortoise-shell, when pierced and burnt in a particular way, seems to have developed certain shapes or signs which were read by the augurs; while the reeds, on being thrown down, arranged themselves in the form of one or more of the sixty-four diagrams, and the response was interpreted accordingly. Several good examples of this form of divination have been left on record; here is a specimen. One of the feudal princes was visited (B.C. 689) by an augur from the suzerain court of Chow, who carried with him the instrumental paraphernalia of his office, in the shape of the Canon of Changes and the necessary reeds. On being invited by the prince to foretell the fortunes of the latter's heir, the augur proceeded to throw down the reeds, in accordance with custom, and found that they arranged themselves on the ground in the form (1) of the diagram *kuan* (the literal meaning of which is "to see," and which is made up of two lines and one divided line over three divided lines), and (2) in the form of the diagram *p'ei* (literally "great," and made up of three lines over three divided lines). The augur then referred to the Canon of Changes, under the headings *kuan* and *p'ei*, and discovered from the interpretations given there that the boy would become ruler of his father's State, or, alternatively, of another State; also, that if he did not become ruler himself in either of the two cases just mentioned, then it was to be anticipated that at least one of his descendants would do so. The two diagrams were further analysed into their component parts, earth and sun, sky and wind. From the former pair it was gathered that the boy would have all the treasures hidden in mountains and be shone upon by the bright sun; in other words, rise to high position. Whereas the presence of wind in the second pair—an essentially moving and unstable element—introduced the possibility of his rise to power in another State than his own.

Sometimes, however, the augur was precluded by the very nature of the question from taking refuge in an ambiguous response. For instance, on one occasion an augur was consulted as to the sex of an unborn child. He divined by the tortoise-shell, and found that the child would be a boy and that his name would be Yu, "friend." He was right. A boy was born, who bore on the palm of his hand a mark, which on examination turned out to be the common character for "friend."

In another case, the advice of an augur, who had been called upon to predict the upshot of a campaign, was altogether set aside, with disastrous results to the commander, who thus ventured to disregard what was considered to be the voice of God.

The following, too, is not without interest. In 642 B.C. five large stones fell from the sky, and six fish-hawks were seen to fly backwards. The reigning prince of the Sung State, where these events took place, inquired of an augur, who was visiting that State, what might be the meaning of these phenomena; and he was told that there would be during that year many deaths in the State of Lu; also that he himself would obtain, for a time, the hegemony of all the States. On leaving the presence, however, the augur said, "The prince had no business to ask me that question. Natural phenomena do not bring with them either good fortune or bad; these are brought about by men themselves. But I did not dare to affront the prince."

As to divination with grain, we are still more in doubt as to the actual process. The ode in which this method is mentioned refers to a time of political trouble from misgovernment, and records the words of one who advises caution and strict adherence to virtuous conduct:

> Men who are grave and wise
> Are temperate in their use of wine;
> But those who are benighted and ignorant,
> Daily give way more and more to drink.
> Be careful, each of you, of your conduct,
> For the grace of God is not conferred twice.
> With a handful of grain I go out and divine
> How I may be able to become good.

Sir J. G. Frazer, in *The Golden Bough*, likens the course of human thought to a web woven of three different threads—the black thread of magic, the red thread of religion, and the white thread of science, the term science standing here for those simple truths drawn from observation of nature, of which men in all ages have possessed a store. He says:

Could we then survey the web of thought from the beginning, we should probably perceive it to be at first a chequer of black and white, a patchwork of true and false notions, hardly tinged as yet by the red thread of religion. But carry your eye further along the fabric and you will remark that, while the black and white chequer still runs through it, there rests on the middle portion of the web, where religion has entered most deeply into its texture, a dark crimson stain which shades off insensibly into a lighter tint as the white thread of science is woven more and more into the tissue.

It does not appear, from the sources of information available to us, that magic, under which head we may include divination, preceded the early religious notions of the Chinese people, though of course this may be due either to the inadequacy of the sources or to inability to interpret them rightly; on the other hand, it may be asserted without fear of contradiction that the ultimate weakening of the religious tint in China was not due to the admixture of science, but to quite another cause, to which I shall hope to come in due time.

Of all the Panegyrics, perhaps the most interesting is that one which relates how the early rulers of the Chow people commended themselves to God by their righteous deeds in the administration of government, and how the divine favour ultimately raised King Wu to the leadership of the federated States.

> How great is God,
> Manifesting His majesty upon earth!
> He surveyed the four quarters of the empire,
> Seeking for someone to give peace to the people.
> The Hsia and the Shang dynasties of old
> Had failed to satisfy Him with their government;
> So throughout the various States
> There was searching and considering
> Until God fixed on the man.

This man was a vigorous chieftain who made clearances for the settlers and enabled them to defeat and scatter the wild tribes around them. The next chieftain was one of his younger sons.

> Gifted by God with the power of judgment,
> So that the fame of his virtue silently grew,

> Able to lead, able to rule—
> To rule over this great country.

He was the father of King Wên—to call the latter by his posthumous title; for, as already stated, he never actually reigned, but like Genghis Khan and the three next Emperors of the Mongol dynasty, he was canonized by a filial descendant. We are now told that, as to King Wên, while ruler over the Chow people in their tribal days,

> His virtue left nothing to be desired,

and that

> He received the blessing of God.

So far, we are on conventional lines, but a new departure is taken in this ode when we are told that

God actually held personal conversations with King Wên, addressing him as follows:

> God said to King Wên,
> Do not be like those who reject this and cling to that;
> Be not like those who are ruled by their desires.

The first result of this injunction was that a mere display of force proved sufficient to win over an unfriendly and aggressive tribe, without recourse to actual hostilities and bloodshed. Then

> God said to King Wên,
> I am pleased with your intelligent virtue,
> Not loudly proclaimed nor obtrusively displayed,
> Without extravagance or vacillation,
> Without consciousness of effort,
> In accordance with My regulations.

Again God said to King Wên:

> Take measures for opposing your enemies,
> Uniting with brother rulers of other States.

> Get ready your scaling-ladders,
> And your storeyed towers (*turres*),
> To attack the walls of Ch'ung.

The narrative continues:

> The storeyed towers were quietly advanced
> Against the lofty and massive walls of Ch'ung;
> Captives were brought in one after another,
> Together with the left ears of the slain.
> At starting, King Wên had sacrificed to God and to the heroes of old,
> Thus seeking to induce submission;
> And throughout the four quarters no one dared to insult him.

Here we have touches which to my mind are distinctly reminiscent of the God of the Old Testament, as seen leading on His chosen people to battle, stimulating their enthusiasm and so achieving victory, not necessarily, as the French cynic would have it, because on the side of the bigger battalions. But we are left entirely in the dark as to how and when and where King Wên received these communications from God; whether he saw Him in person, or whether, as in the case of Moses, he hid his face, afraid to look upon the divine glory.

B.C. 1200-500

THE Chows, of whom so much has already been said, chiefly as a tribal community before they secured, under King Wu (1122 B.C.), the hegemony of the feudal States, traced their line back to a personage, called Hou Chi, deified, so soon as the Chows obtained supreme power, as the Consort of God. His date was about 2500 B.C. His real name was Castaway, given to him because more than one attempt was made to get rid of him, some say as a thing of ill omen. For his was indeed a miraculous birth, even if not, as supposed by many, a genuinely virgin birth, to dispose of which view it has been found necessary to drag in an early Emperor as the putative husband of his mother, Chiang Yüan. After these few introductory words, the ode now to be quoted will be found to tell its own tale in sufficiently intelligible terms:

>The origin of our people
>Dates from Chiang Yüan.
>How did she accomplish this?
>She reverently offered up sacrifice
>That she might not be without children. p. 34
>Then she stepped in a footprint made by God, and conceived,
>As there, all alone, she stood still.
>Pregnancy followed; in due season
>She gave birth to, and suckled,
>Him whom men now call Hou Chi.
>When she had fulfilled her months,
>Her first-born came like a lamb;
>There was no tearing, no rending,
>No injury, no pain,
>In order to emphasize his divinity.
>Did not God give her comfort?
>Had He not accepted her reverent sacrifice,
>So that thus easily she brought forth her son?

After the above extraordinary incidents, in which it is competent to anyone to detect or to denounce evidence of parthenogenesis and also of supernatural manifestations, we may not be altogether astonished to find that the babe, instead of being warmly received, was on the contrary "despised and rejected of men." This would be entirely in keeping with Chinese views on such subjects, ancient and modern alike; not that any simple claim to divinity of origin would ever be seriously resented by the Chinese people, who would simply believe or disbelieve according to the temperament of each individual, but because, whether supernatural or not, such a birth would at any rate be unnatural, and therefore repugnant to the feelings of a nation to which uniformity of procedure, especially as regards the operation of natural laws, is the criterion of what is right. Several plots were directed against the life of Hou Chi, as detailed in the ode:

> He was exposed in a narrow lane,
> But sheep and oxen protected and suckled him.
> He was exposed in a forest,
> But some wood-cutters found him.
> He was exposed on cold ice,
> But a bird covered him with its wings.
> When the bird flew away,
> Hou Chi began to wail;
> He cried loud and long,
> So that he was heard all down the road.

Hou Chi devoted himself, in the interests of his countrymen, to agriculture, and at the date of this ode, which of course cannot be older than the twelfth century B.C., was still worshipped as the Father of Husbandry. At the same time, in view of the profound feelings of veneration and affection which his personality aroused in the hearts of his countrymen, it was specially laid down that his spirit was not to be allowed to take precedence of God.

The concluding lines of this panegyric are important for their bearing on sacrifice, a phase of religion on which, so far, we have but slightly touched. Hou Chi himself, we are told, had established the custom of offering up sacrifices of grain—a primitive form of the Harvest Festival, or Thanksgiving; but now the writer of the ode asks,

> How shall we arrange our sacrifices to Hou Chi?
> Some rub grain in the mortar, others scoop it out,

> Some sift it, some tread it from the husk,
> Some wash it—*sou*, *sou* (suggesting noise),
> Some steam it *fou*, *fou* (suggesting steam).
> Now we divine, now we consider the ceremonial.
> We burn fragrant southernwood together with the fat of the victim;
> We take a ram, and offer it in sacrifice;
> We offer roast flesh and broiled;
> And thus welcome the New Year.

I must interrupt these closing verses to say that the line which I have translated

> We take a ram, and offer it in sacrifice,

and which may be compared with "the ram of consecration" (Exodus xxix. 31), is declared by commentators to mean

> We sacrifice a ram to the Spirit of the Path.

This is mere guesswork on the part of Chinese scholars. The word, used here for the first and only time in the genuinely ancient Canon, is said to mean a sacrifice at starting on a journey, which would have no application in the present connexion. By the time this ode was written, there may well have been a God of the Road, invoked for safe journeys; but it seems simpler here to keep the idea of sacrifice without insisting on a minor deity. The panegyric ends with the following lines:

> We pile the wooden sacrificial vessels with meat,
> And fill the earthenware vessels with broth.
> At length the fragrance mounts on high,
> And God, well pleased, smells the sweet savour,
> Sweet indeed, and in due season.

The coincidence between the last line but one and Genesis viii. 21, where "the Lord smelled a sweet savour" arising from Noah's burnt offering, and promised to curse the earth no more, is sufficiently remarkable; it is further interesting to note the comment on the words of the Old Testament by Dr Waterland, the distinguished theologian and Master of Magdalene College, Cambridge, from 1713 to 1740.

This expression is used in great condescension to human thoughts and human language; and is intended to signify that God was pleased with the piety and devout services of Noah and others, sacrificing to Him from a pure heart, as men are wont to be pleased with sweet odours. A comparison taken from things human serves in some measure to illustrate things divine; and though it is not exact, as none can be exact, yet it helps to convey a more lively and more affecting idea of the thing than could be given without it.

It remains to add that the Chinese term used is *Shang Ti* and not *T'ien*, bearing out a distinction I have attempted to establish between these two expressions, which are beyond all doubt names for one and the same Being. *T'ien* may be regarded as God Passive, *Shang Ti* as God Active; *T'ien* as Jahveh, or Jehovah (in spite of Dr Pusey's prohibition of these forms), *Shang Ti* as God. *T'ien* is perhaps more an abstract, *Shang Ti* a more personal Deity. Reference to *T'ien* is usually associated with fate or destiny, calamities, blessings, prayers for help, and so forth. The commandments of *T'ien* are hard to obey. He is compassionate, as well as to be feared, unjust, and cruel. *Shang Ti* is more definitely associated with a heaven for departed spirits, and He walks, as God did in the Garden of Eden, leaves tracks on the ground, enjoys, as we have seen, the sweet savour of sacrifices, approves or disapproves of conduct, deals with rewards or punishments in a more intimate way, and comes more actually into touch with the human race. After all, these are but varying aspects of one Deity, the two forming a Duality in Unity—two Persons in one God, each of whom is Almighty, though there are not two Almighties; to borrow the words attributed to Saint Athanasius, "neither afore, or after other: neither greater, or less than another."

With the quotation of one more short ode, running only to eight lines, we may take final leave of Hou Chi. This ode is noteworthy (1) for its language as a prayer, and (2) for the varying interpretations which have been discovered of its text.

> O thou divine one, Hou Chi,
> Fit peer of God,
> Establish our myriad people;
> There is none greater than thou.
> Give us this day our wheat and barley,
> Which God appointed for the nourishment of all;

And without distinction of frontier or boundary,
Diffuse all virtues throughout this great land.

There is a singular passage in Chuang Tzǔ, the Taoist writer of the fourth and third centuries B.C., who will shortly claim our attention, which passage has nothing to do with Taoism, but has passed, like many other sayings of the kind, into popular usage. The Emperor Yao, who, as we have already seen, abdicated in favour of the peasant Shun, is said to have previously wished to abdicate in favour of Hsü Yu, a worthy hermit of the day, and to have addressed him accordingly. But the hermit replied,

"If a cook is unable to dress his funeral sacrifices, the boy who impersonates the dead may not step over the wines and meats and do it for him."

It is with the impersonator of the dead that we now have to deal, references to whom go back to the very earliest ages. This impersonator appears to have been a youth, who was introduced into ancestral worship, not merely as a representative of the dead hero or ancestor in whose honour the sacrifice was offered, but as a body in which the dead man's spirit could find an abiding-place, enabling it to be present among the worshippers. The illusion was enhanced by an absolute muteness and immobility on the part of the boy; hence the appositeness of Chuang Tzǔ's remark, If a cook is unable to dress his funeral sacrifices, the boy who impersonates the dead may not step over the wines and meats and do it for him."

The phrase "impersonator of the dead" occurs twice in the Canon of History, both times as a term of contempt, suggesting indolence of an extreme type. It is used of T'ai K'ang, third Emperor of the Hsia dynasty, who came to the throne in 2188 B.C., as follows: "T'ai K'ang occupied the throne like an impersonator of the dead. By idleness and dissipation he extinguished his virtue, until the black-haired people all began to waver in their allegiance." But it is to the Odes that we must turn to find a fairly complete picture of this ancient ceremonial worship. After storing up grain of various kinds, distilling rice-whisky, and preparing various meats, the intending worshippers, "seeking to increase their own bright happiness," induct the impersonator, and

With correct and reverent deportment,
The oxen and sheep all pure,

> Proceed to the winter or autumnal sacrifices.
> Some flay the victims, some boil the flesh;
> The celebrant (literally, the one who prays) sacrifices within the temple gate,
> And the rites are brilliantly carried through.
> Now are present our glorious ancestors,
> Whose spirits quietly enjoy the offerings,
> While their filial descendants
> Will receive many blessings,
> And be rewarded, to their great happiness,
> With life everlasting, without end.

The next stage is the banquet, reserved, with the exception of a loving-cup, for the spirits only. There are large dishes of roast and broiled meats, and many other smaller dishes, in the preparation of which the women of the family are reverently employed. The loving-cup goes round, and all drink.

> Every form is according to rule;
> Every word and every smile are as they should be.

Finally, when the worshippers and guests are thoroughly exhausted, every detail of the ceremonial having been strictly performed, we are told that the celebrant makes the following announcement:

> Fragrant has been your filial sacrifice,
> And the spirits have enjoyed the wine and food;
> They confer on you all possible blessings,
> Such as you desire, in accordance with custom.

Bells and drums then warn the company that the ceremony is at an end. The celebrant makes one last, and to our ears strange announcement:

> The Spirits are all drunk,

upon which the impersonator of the dead rises from his seat, and, amid the clash of bells and the roll of drums, withdraws from the scene. Simultaneously, of course, the spirits cease to inform those temporary tenements of clay; they evanesce, and are gone, no one knows whither.

The spiritual banquet being now over, worshippers and guests, together with the impersonator of the dead, throw off restraint and proceed to enjoy the more material banquet, at which the funeral baked meats amply furnish forth the dining-tables. It is true that by a pleasant fiction the spirits have extracted from these meats, for their own enjoyment, most of their delicate flavour; still, to judge by the last verse of the ode we have been quoting, enough, and to spare, has remained.

> The musical instruments are brought in for playing,
> In order to add a charm to this second feast;
> The dishes of food are set forth;
> There is no grumbling, but all feel happy.
> When drunk, and satiated with food,
> Great and small bow their heads, and the celebrant says,
> The spirits have enjoyed your wine and food,
> And will bestow on you long life;
> Your sacrifices, all in due season,
> Have been fully performed by you.
> May your sons and your grandsons
> Never fail to do likewise.

We have now nearly done with the Odes, the chief source of all that we really know, or can infer, of the ancient religion of the Chinese. There still remains, however, a certain attitude of man towards the Deity, already touched upon, which finds its place in these early records, just as we can trace, more faintly perhaps, the murmurings of the Jews in some of the books of the Old Testament. This attitude is one of dissatisfaction with the dispensations of Providence; a dissatisfaction often carried to open resentment, and expressed in stronger language than was ever used, so far as we can see, in the murmurings of the children of Israel. Thus we have such lines as,

> God is sending down calamities,
> God is acting oppressively,
> God is getting angry.

Again:

> What wrong have we done now,
> That God sends down death and disorder?

There is indeed one case in which an epithet applied to the Deity seems translatable only by some such word as "hide-bound," in the sense of strict and unnecessary adherence to the letter rather than to the spirit. The value of the Chinese word in question may be gauged by its application to blocks cut for printing, where it is the equivalent of our term "stereotyped." In some of the Odes, however, a different note is struck; one of obedience and resignation to the heavenly will. Thus we have,

> Almighty God makes no mistakes,

and then a whole verse, as follows:

> Revere the anger of God,
> And venture not to make light of it; p. 43
> Revere the changing moods of God,
> And venture not to pursue your own course.
> Almighty God sees clearly,
> And is with you in your outgoings.
> Almighty God is discerning,
> And is with you in all your wanderings.

The next important source of information on early religious sentiments in China dates from about the beginning of the genuinely historical period, and requires a brief introduction.

In addition to the works which Confucius edited, he undertook to write up the annals of his native State from the year 721 B.C. These annals, as they stand, consist entirely of bald entries of events, and would be of little use or interest to anyone but for their association with a famous commentary in which many of the events recorded are treated in detail, showing the circumstances which led up to them, and the consequences which distinguished them from mere everyday happenings. This commentary is supposed to have been written by a disciple, named Tso-ch'iu Ming, some say under the guidance of Confucius, if even not actually by Confucius himself. It would be impossible, in anything short of a whole lecture, to deal with the literary question here involved; or to give a faint idea of the dramatic incidents related, or of the fascinating style of the writer—a blend of Tacitean terseness with "Livy's picture page." It must suffice to say that Confucius wrote the annals, entitled the "Springs and Autumns" in reference to the arrangement of the entries under the four seasons of the year; and that someone wrote the commentary, to which I now ask your attention.

Throughout the annals and the commentary alike, the king of the Chow State, who was suzerain as compared with the rulers of the vassal States, is invariably spoken of in this connexion as God's king, or as we should put it, king by the grace of God; in a more general sense, as the delegated arbiter of human destinies, he was known as God's son, a term which was still in existence until a couple of years ago, and which for obvious reasons, as before stated, has been modified into the Son of Heaven. The intervention of God Himself in the current affairs of men was firmly believed in, and is alluded to again and again in terms of the simplest faith. "God has rid them of that pestilent fellow," says one; "God does not employ men who walk on tiptoe," meaning by this strange figure of speech persons inclined to pass jauntily through the gravest crisis. "Duplicity," we are told, "is contrary to the ordinances of God"; but failing any revealed commandment to that effect, we have no alternative but to class these utterances as intuitions of the writer. They remind us, indeed, of similar remarks by our own bishops and priests, who often declare, with a somewhat reprehensible familiarity, that God likes, or dislikes, this, that, or the other.

The value of an oath was greatly enhanced by calling God to witness. There would be a solemn sacrifice in a temple, and an oath would be taken, of which this is an actual example: "If I am not loyal to my prince and to those who are working for the good of our country—may God deal with me!" At the conclusion of the oath it was customary for the covenanter to smear his lips with the blood of the victim. One example is given of a treaty which had been extracted by force; and the commentary says that such a treaty might well have been disregarded, at the same time eulogizing the man who would not repudiate his oath, even though unfairly obtained. A further example, recorded in the year 494, tells us of a man who promised to kill his prince's mother, at a given signal from the prince. This plot he failed to carry out; explaining that he only agreed to do so through fear for his own life, and adding, in anticipation of Paley, that only such promises should be kept as could be justly and rightly performed.

The life of Confucius furnishes us with another illustration. He had been taken prisoner by rebels, and was released on condition of not proceeding to the Wei State. Thither, notwithstanding, he continued his route; and when asked by a disciple whether it was right to violate his oath, he replied, "It was a forced oath; the spirits do not recognize such." One more example of these old-world beliefs. A treaty of peace having been concluded (B.C. 589) with the eastern tribes, a princelet suggested attacking them while off their guard. To this the Grand Augur said, "The violation of a treaty will bring you bad luck. Neither the spirits nor man will help you; how, then, can you expect to succeed?" The princelet went his own way, and suffered a severe defeat.

The fear of God seems to have been ever before the eyes of the Chinese people during the period with which we are now occupied. Of one of the feudal princes a speaker said, "He will not escape his doom. Himself regardless of propriety, he punishes those who observe it. But to practise propriety is to obey the laws of God; propriety is indeed the will of God. A superior man is not harsh either to the young or to the lowly, because he stands in awe of God." The Chinese character here translated by "propriety" is a word of Protean possibilities; it represents one of what we may call the five cardinal virtues of the Confucian moral system, and the application of such a rendering as "propriety" has met with not a little ridicule at the hands of the hasty. For "propriety," according to Murray's New English Dictionary, covers precisely the ground required; e.g., by such definitions of the word as "conformity with rule or principle; rightness; justness; correctness of behaviour or morals." In ordinary Chinese life the word is used to express "politeness and etiquette," but in the classical language its sense may be gathered from the above various meanings of propriety, than which objectors have so far failed to provide a better term.

With regard to any general fear of God, we learn from the earlier records that such fear was limited to evil-doers, whose acts would be contrary to the proper harmony of the universe. Given right conduct on the part of man, there would be no further intervention on the part of God. The question of belief or disbelief in a God hardly seems to have arisen until later ages. In the commentary, however, we do meet with a more openly expressed desire on the part of the Deity to occupy in the hearts of the people a similar position to that of the God of the Old Testament in the hearts of His chosen race. Sacrifices, if duly performed, had always been supposed to avert divine punishment for some irregular act; but here we have references which tell in a different sense. A man dreamed that God sent an angel to him, saying, "Sacrifice to Me, and I will bless thee." This is a striking point, because it was always to the spirits of deceased ancestors that sacrifices were regularly offered, with a view to ensure assistance in time of need. "My sacrifices have always been abundant and pure," said a reigning prince; "the spirits will surely hold me up." To which his minister replied, "I have heard that the spirits, good and evil alike, do not attach themselves to a mere human personality, but are attracted only by the goodness of a man's disposition."

When sacrifices are mentioned in the various records we have been using, it is understood that the victim in each case would be one of the domestic animals, variously enumerated, under B.C. 637, as six, and under B.C. 529 as five. These animals, to adopt the larger number, would be the horse (specially so mentioned under B.C. 563), ox, sheep, fowl, dog, and pig. Under B.C. 637 we read that the ruler of one feudal State insisted upon the ruler of another State offering up in sacrifice the ruler of a third State, in order, as we are told, to awe certain wild tribes which had been giving trouble. A minister, too late to save the victim, spoke as follows: "Of old, the six domestic animals were not sacrificed indifferently, one for another; neither for small matters were large animals used. How much less, then, would human beings have been taken as victims? Sacrifices are offered for the benefit of men. Men are the hosts, and spirits are the guests. If you sacrifice a man, who will enjoy it? Our ruler, at his assembly of the feudal princes, has treated with oppression the rulers of two other States, and has further used one of them in sacrifice to a disgusting and unrecognized spirit. Will it not be difficult to secure the hegemony of the States in this way? Our ruler will be lucky if he dies in his bed."

A little more than one hundred years later, B.C. 529, we read that the prince of the Ch'u State succeeded in extinguishing the Ts'ai State, and sacrificed the eldest son of his vanquished rival. Even if the sacrifice of human beings, in the usual acceptance of the term, was not widely practised, we know that both men and women were often buried alive as companions to the dead. Under B.C. 590 we have an account of the burial of a feudal ruler, who had governed badly and had wasted the resources of his State upon improper objects. His two chief ministers gave him an extravagant funeral, using lime made from burnt oyster-shells (as extracted at the present day) for lining the inside of the grave, and having more than the usual number of carriages and horses, for which they were duly censured by the "superior man," who is here supposed to be none other than the writer of the commentary himself. Then, as we are told, "for the first time men were buried alive with the corpse." There must, however, be something wrong either with the text or its interpretation; for under the year B.C. 618 we already have this earlier allusion to the custom: "When the Duke Mu, the ruler of the Chin State, died, three brothers were buried alive with him. They were all good men, and their fellow-countrymen mourned their loss in the ode called the Yellow Birds, which was specially composed to their memory."

Turning to the ode in question, we find it to consist of three stanzas, all in exactly the same strain, but with a different brother commemorated in each. It will suffice, therefore, to quote a single stanza:

> They flit about, those yellow birds,
> And rest upon the jujube tree.

I may explain that it is customary, especially in Chinese lyrical poetry, to prefix some such lines, the application of which is not always obvious. In the present case, each stanza opens with the two lines given above, but no two critics agree as to their right interpretation. The rest is simple enough.

> Who followed Duke Mu into the grave?
> Yen-hsi, the son of Tzŭ-chü.
> Ah, this Yen-hsi
> Was one in a hundred.
> When he came to the grave
> He looked terrified and trembled. p. 50
> O God, Thou in the blue,
> Thou art destroying our good men.
> Could he have been ransomed,
> We would have given a hundred lives for his.

The line

> O God, Thou in the blue,

reminds me that at the present day, when the idea of God has faded in China to little more than a name, He is still occasionally spoken of as the Wearer of the Blue Clothes.

In another case, one of the feudal princes, seeing that some mess had been made in his courtyard, fell down in a fit of passion upon a charcoal brazier, and was so badly burnt that he died. Five chariots with their teams of horses, together with five men, were buried alive in his honour. The historian quaintly adds that his death was due, partly to his violent temper and partly to his love of cleanliness.

A writer of the fourth century B.C. relates how and when the custom of burying alive became unpopular with the Chinese people.

"A certain man having died, his wife and steward took counsel together as to who should be buried with him. All was settled before the arrival of his brother (a well-known disciple of Confucius); and then they informed him, saying, 'We must ask you to go down with the body into the grave.' 'Burial of the living with the dead,' replied the brother, 'is not in accordance with established rites. Still, as you say that someone is wanted to attend upon the deceased, who better fitted than his wife and steward? If this contingency can be avoided altogether, I am willing; but if not, then the duty will devolve upon you two.' From that time forth the custom fell into desuetude."

In spite of this last statement, we know that at the grand funeral of the so-called First Emperor, in B.C. 210, all his concubines were buried alive in the magnificent mausoleum where his body was laid, as well as all the workmen who had constructed it and knew the secret of its treasures; the workmen, of course, not from any religious motive.

To return to natural phenomena, which have at all times entered very largely into the religious beliefs of the Chinese, and may be said to do so even at the present day, when gongs and cymbals are still beaten to prevent a great dog from swallowing the sun or moon at eclipse time. There is a passage in the Canon of History which is understood, no doubt rightly, to refer to an eclipse. The two Grand Astronomers, appointed under the Emperor Yao, had been neglecting their duties and giving way to intemperance. Then there suddenly occurred what we may call a "celestial failure"; the blind musicians beat their drums; officials and people hurried wildly about; while the two Grand Astronomers behaved like mere impersonators of the dead. Grand Astronomers had in those days an uneasy billet; the penalty for antedating or postdating an eclipse was, in both cases, death.

Eclipses are only mentioned once in the Odes, at a very early date, which has been carefully verified. The term used was then composed of the word "eat," and either "sun" or "moon," as required. On the 29th of August, B.C. 775, says an ode,

> The sun was eclipsed
> A thing of very evil omen.
> First the moon looked small,
> And then the sun looked small.
> Henceforth the people
> Will be pitiable indeed.
> The sun and moon presage evil
> By not keeping to their proper paths;
> All through the kingdom there is no government,
> Because good men are not employed.
> For the moon to be eclipsed Is a small matter;
> But now that the sun has been eclipsed,
> How dreadful is that!

On the 20th April, B.C. 610, another eclipse of the sun took place. This is not the first instance recorded in the "Springs and Autumns," but the remarks of the commentary are more conveniently arranged for quotation. The writer says, "On the occasion of an eclipse of the sun, the Son of Heaven should not have his table spread so lavishly as usual, and should have drums beaten at the altar to the spirits of the land, while the feudal princes should present offerings of silk to the spirits of the land and have drums beaten at their courts, thus manifesting their own service of the spirits and so teaching the people to serve their rulers, according to the respective rights of each, as was customary in ancient days."

It is obvious that an eclipse was regarded as a threatening notification from on high, vague though the message may have been. Still more so was this the case with comets, of which a large number have been recorded in Chinese history. In B.C. 524 a comet appeared, travelling eastward towards the Milky Way. An official said, "This is a broom, to sweep away the old and give us new. God often makes use of such signs. The feudal princes will suffer from calamities by fire." It was then suggested to the Prime Minister of the Chêng State that the danger should be averted, so far as Chêng was concerned, by offering, presumably to God, valuable goblets of jade and some other precious stone; but this proposal was rejected.

Drought had always been regarded as a divine visitation, and sacrifices and prayers for rain were as common in ancient days as they are at present. In B.C. 637 there was a serious drought in the Lu State. The reigning prince wished to burn a witch as a propitiatory sacrifice; but a minister said, "No, that is not a proper course to take. Rather put your city walls into good repair; spend less on your table, and be economical in your general expenditure. Exalt thrift and urge the people to help one another. That is the right course to take. What has a witch to do with the matter? If God now wishes her to die, why did He ever give her life? If she can really produce drought, to burn her will only increase the calamity." The witch's life was spared, and that year there was not great scarcity of food.

Famines were divided into five classes of intensity, based upon the number of the five kinds of grain which happened to be affected. A famine of the worst kind, when all the five grains were more or less ruined by drought, entailed various inconveniences upon the prince. From another commentary by another writer (Ku-liang) we learn that he should not be served with two dishes at once, nor renew the plaster on his towers and terraces; that he should discontinue his archery feasts, and leave the road to the archery ground uncared for; that certain offices should be maintained, but nothing done in them; and that the spirits should be prayed to, but no sacrifices offered.

Floods, the result of too much rain, were naturally as much dreaded as drought. In B.C. 681 there were bad floods in the Sung State. The prince of Lu was sent to condole, saying, "God has visited cruel rains upon you, which will lessen your supply of millet for sacrifice. I cannot but offer you my sympathy." "I am an orphan," was the reply, "and wanting in reverence; therefore God has sent this calamity upon me. For the sorrow I have caused you, I beg to express my regrets." It is added that the use of the term "orphan" is proper for the ruler of a State which is overtaken by misfortune, but no further explanation is given. The reference is probably to the alienation of God, his father.

Locusts have always been one of the plagues of China, and there is quite a literature on the various methods for getting rid of this pest. In B.C. 623 we are told that locusts fell from the sky like rain, being, happily, killed by the fall. The annals of China contain entries of many extraordinary rains, such as blood, gold, millet, hair, grass, pieces of flesh, ashes, earth, pigs, fishes, beans, frogs, paper money, iron, and other things. We know now that some of these entries are anything but ridiculous, being easily explained by the action of whirlwinds, which pick up at one spot and drop at another, too far off for the limited communications available in early years. One night in September 1912—I am quoting from the *London and China Telegraph*—

Hundreds of Chinese in Shanghai profoundly believed that a miracle was happening before their eyes. It rained rice, which fell in little showers, and from 10 o'clock until long after midnight groups of natives were on hands and knees scraping over roadways and gutters for a grain or two. The remarkable phenomenon is explained by the typhoon which has just touched on Shanghai. It is suggested that the typhoon destroyed a granary, the grains of rice being whirled high up in the heavens, carried by strong currents to distant places, falling as the force of the winds abated.

Raining blood, too, has been satisfactorily accounted for by the presence of a red secretion, chiefly from the pupal chrysalis of a certain butterfly (genus *Vanessa*); as to several of the other entries, we may follow the Confucian maxim: "Hear much, and put aside those points on which you are in doubt."

Earthquakes were very naturally supposed to proceed from supernatural agencies. One writer says, "It is the way of the earth to be still; its moving was accounted strange, and was therefore recorded." Another declares that an earthquake is "nature's response to prevailing disorder in the kingdom, the feudal princes disobedient to the Son of Heaven, and their officers disobedient to them." When, therefore, in B.C. 518, a high official perished in a severe shock, it was simply remarked that God had done with him. He was killed, as he might equally well have been killed for his misdeeds, at a later date, by thunder. I say "at a later date," for it does not appear from any of the older books of the Canon that thunder, though dreaded, was used either by or on behalf of God as an instrument of punishment for the wickedness of man. We shall return to this in another connexion.

Among other natural phenomena which the Chinese regard with uncertainty and fear, must be classed the rainbow. The literati of China have not been able to make much out of it, and confine themselves to saying that its appearance is due to some irregularity in nature. It is of evil omen, and portends fighting. Two lines in the Odes say,

> There is a rainbow in the east;
> Do not venture to point at it.

For pointing at a rainbow is thought to produce sores on the hands. No one can say precisely who is offended by the act of pointing; whether it be the Deity Himself, or some spirit, good or evil, who may be appointed to the stewardship of rainbows.

Here we may, perhaps opportunely, devote some attention to the term "spirit," which has been so frequently used in reference to beings, if not of another world like ours, as the Chinese now believe, at any rate of an unseen world. In all ages, spirits have been divided by the Chinese into two classes, good and bad spirits, otherwise known as spirits and devils. Departed heroes, and personal relatives and friends, supply the former class, but it is not so easy to show how the latter came into existence. It is a mere guess to say that they are the souls of wicked persons; there is no authority for such a statement, except in the case of wandering spirits from the unburied corpses of wicked persons. However this may be, it has always been understood that diseases are brought about by evil spirits; more than this, a disease is actually personified as an evil spirit, and is exorcised from a patient, or driven from a village, by incantations, clanging of gongs, and similar ceremonies. We read in the commentary, B.C. 541, that when a certain feudal prince was ill, the divining officer declared that his disease was caused by two spirits, of whom the Grand Augur had never heard. However, the Prime Minister of a friendly State, who had come with "kind inquiries," showed that the two spirits in question presided over a star and a district respectively, and were necessarily harmless. "The spirits of the hills and streams," he explained, "are sacrificed to in times of flood, drought, and pestilence. The spirits of the sun, moon, and stars are sacrificed to on the unseasonable occurrence of snow, hoar-frost, wind, or rain. Your Highness must be suffering from something connected with your outgoings or incomings, with your food, with your griefs or joys. What can these spirits of the mountains and stars have to do with it?"

Nothing, indeed, as matters turned out; the disease was traced to the fact that four of the ladies of the harem bore the same surname as the prince himself. Marriage between persons of the same surname has always, with certain special exceptions, been forbidden in China; in this case it was held that the rule extended to relations with concubines as well.

Already, as we have seen, the worship of God and of the departed spirits of human beings had been enlarged to include spirits assigned to such inanimate objects as hills and trees. In B.C. 563 a feudal prince, bent, as usual, upon a marauding expedition, had occasion to cross the Yellow River. There was a pause; two pairs of jade tablets were bound together by a thread of red silk, and a prayer was offered up, showing the supposed righteousness of the campaign, and closing with these words: "If the enterprise be crowned with success, there will be no disgrace attaching to you, O ye spirits of the river. Do you, therefore, decide." Then the jade was dropped into the stream, and the prince crossed over.

In all worship of spirits, faith was the essential. We have the record of a minister explaining to his prince that a small State could only contend against a large State if the former were governed according to the rule of right, while the latter was abandoned to wild excesses. "What I mean," he said, "by rule of right is a loyal care for the people on the part of the authorities, and faith in the spirits on the part of the priests and augurs. Just now, our people are famishing; the prince gives way to his passions, and the priests are but hypocrites in their performance of the sacrifices." To this the prince replied that his sacrificial animals were of the best kind and well fattened, and that the millet he used was good and abundant. "Where," he inquired, "is there any lack of faith?" "The spirits," rejoined the minister, "consider the welfare of the people first, and religious ceremonial second. Consequently, when our virtuous rulers of old offered up fat animals, it meant that their people were fat also; the spirits showered blessings upon them, and they were successful in all their undertakings."

Good spirits are usually regarded as invisible, though instances have been known, in more modern times, of spirits mixing with ordinary people, and being distinguishable only by the fact that their apparent bodies cast no shadow. Evil spirits, in the form of horrid goblins, have often been seen in China as elsewhere. In 660 B.C. a spirit actually came down—"came down" are the words used—and settled in the Kuo State. The suzerain, or king of the Chow State, asked his Grand Augur what this arrival might portend; to which the Augur made the following reply: When the prosperity of a State is increasing, good spirits come down to take note of its virtuous adminis- tration; similarly, when a State is about to perish, spirits also come down to watch its evil administration. So that the arrival of spirits has sometimes been followed by prosperity, sometimes by the reverse." The king then commissioned his Augur to proceed to the Kuo State, bearing the proper offerings to the spirit. There the Augur heard that the prince of Kuo was trying to get the spirit to grant him an enlargement of territory, of course at some other State's expense. The spirit stayed in the Kuo State for six months; and after receiving many prayers and sacrifices, finally promised the coveted accession of territory. Thereupon, the Augur predicted the downfall of the Kuo State, saying, "I have heard that when the prosperity of a country is increasing, it is because the prince gives ear to the people; and that when a State is about to perish, it is because the prince gives ear to spirits."

It would be of surpassing interest to know exactly what was in the minds of the ancient Chinese when they spoke of spirits, and especially what was the exact connotation of the phrase "came down" as applied to spirits. Where did they come down from, and what was the nature of the place they left by so coming, and of its other inhabitants? Were they attendants upon God, in a state of happiness, and subject to His commandments? We know from a passage in the commentary, that under the Chow dynasty, as already mentioned, God took precedence of all spirits, including that of Hou Chi, the divine founder of the House of Chow. Let us now see what more the commentary may have to divulge on the shadowy question of the soul.

In B.C. 542 there died a wild, hard-drinking individual, named Po-yu, who had been obliged to flee from his home for political reasons which are of no importance here. Some few years later, a report spread about that Po-yu was alive and had been seen by several persons, to whom he had used threatening remarks about others. This created a small panic; so that when people met together, if anyone said, "Here's Po-yu!" there would be a general stampede in all directions, "no one quite knowing," as the commentary tells us, "where he was going to." The excitement reached its climax when one of the threatened persons died; then the Prime Minister intervened, and made arrangements by which the fears of the populace were allayed. He explained that if a disembodied spirit has a place to go to, it does not become an evil spirit," and that he had now provided a proper refuge for Po-yu's spirit, thereby bringing the manifestations to an end. Later on, he was asked if he really believed that Po-yu could become a disembodied spirit; in other words, if he believed in spirits at all. "It is quite possible," he replied. "When a man is born, what he first develops is called *p'o* (answering to what is now known as the supraliminal soul); then follows the male, or positive, of the *p'o*, which is called *hun* (the subliminal soul). By drawing from its environment what is essential, this joint soul becomes strong, and finally active. With regard to the manifestations of spirits, if an ordinary man or woman dies, this joint soul can still keep hanging about in the form of an evil apparition; still more would this be so in the case of such a man as Po-yu."

Thus we have, five hundred years before Christ, a simple statement that there was such a thing as a soul, that it was of a twofold character, and could remain in the world after the death and disappearance of the body to which it had belonged. How this view was further expanded in scope as time went on, and overlaid with a variety of fantastic beliefs, will be more appropriately dealt with when we come to a later period of religious development in China.

In addition to the chief commentary on the "Springs and Autumns," from which most of the above details have been gleaned, two other commentaries of considerable, but not of such surpassing value have come down to us. There is a short note on "Praying for Rain " by one of these commentators (already mentioned), named Ku-Jiang, which is perhaps worth quoting. "Prayers for rain should be offered up in spring and summer only; not in autumn or winter. Why not in autumn or winter? Because the moisture of growing things is not then exhausted; neither has man reached the limit of his skill. Why in spring and summer? Because time is then pressing, and man's skill is of no further avail. How so? Because without rain just then, nothing could be made to grow; the crops would fail, and famine would ensue. But why wait until time is pressing, and man's skill is of no further avail? Because prayers for rain are the same as asking a favour, and the ancients did not lightly ask favours. Why so? Because they held it more blessed to give than to receive; and as the latter excludes the former, the main object of man's life is taken away. How is praying for rain asking a favour? It is a request that God will do something for us. The inspired men of old who had any request to make to God were careful to prefer it in due season. At the head of all his high officers of state, the prince would proceed in person to offer up his prayer. He could not ask anyone else to go as his proxy." The idea here seems to be, and this will be borne out by an example to be cited later on, that improper or unseasonable requests are not to be preferred to God. A native critic adds, "If we are not to ask favours of God, how much less may we ask them of one another. Persons who recklessly ask favours should not be treated with the consideration to which they would otherwise be entitled."

So far we have reviewed in a desultory way—perhaps the only possible way—two important ages in Chinese history: (1) the age of the early, and more or less legendary Emperors, who first ruled, and finally misruled the empire from the beginning of the third to nearly the end of the second millennium B.C.; and (2) the feudal age, from 1122 B.C. down to, roughly speaking, the middle of the sixth century B.C. The feudal age did not, indeed, come to an end at that date; there were still a couple of centuries and more to run before the Chow dynasty collapsed under the overwhelming power of one of the feudal States, the ruler of which became, as he styled himself, the First Emperor of a united China, meaning that "the great procession of the centuries was to begin again" from his reign. The reason why our second period has to end when it does, is that the continuance of the Chow dynasty, or feudal age, amid scenes of rivalry and bloodshed which gained for its last century and a half the distinctive title of the age of the "Fighting States," is of no account whatever as compared with the appearance on the scene of a man who for twenty-five centuries past has been the guiding star of the Chinese people, and whose influence, temporarily obscured during the great political crisis of recent days, is now likely to continue to mould the lives and destinies of his countrymen.

B.C. 500-300

CONFUCIUS was born in the year 551 B.C., and died at the age of seventy-three, after a strenuous career, devoted partly to politics, partly to teaching, and partly to literary research. His own view of his life and achievements was that of a disappointed man. On one occasion he cried out, "Alas! there is no one who knows me." On another, he bewailed the non-appearance of the phœnix, a bird always to be found in countries where right principles prevail; he also complained that divine revelations, such as had occurred in the case of the Eight Diagrams and the River Plan, were no longer vouchsafed. "It is all over with me!" he cried in despair; for he probably believed in both the above manifestations, and regretted that nothing of the kind had been reserved for his own generation. Dr Legge's grand contributions to our knowledge of the Canon are occasionally marred by comments which are out of place in a purely exegetical work. In reference to the above, he inserts four words: "Confucius endorses these fables"—words likely to give great offence to a Confucianist. It is as though a Confucian translator of the Bible, when dealing with the story of Jonah and the whale, were to add, quite unnecessarily, "Christ endorses this fable" (Matthew xii. 40). On a third occasion, Confucius said, "My doctrines make no way; I will get upon a raft and float about on the sea."

Against these pessimistic utterances may be set the eulogy pronounced by the historian, Ssŭ-ma Ch'ien (second and first centuries B.C.): "When reading the works of Confucius, I have always fancied I could see the man as he was in life; and when I went to Shantung I actually beheld his carriage, his robes, and the instrumental parts of his ceremonial usages. There were his descendants practising the old rites in their ancestral home; and I lingered long, unable to tear myself away. Countless are the princes and prophets that the world has seen in its time; glorious in life, forgotten in death. But Confucius, though only a humble member of the cotton-clothed masses, remains among us after many generations. He is the model for such as would be wise. By all, from the Son of Heaven down to the meanest student, the supremacy of his principles is fully and freely admitted. He may indeed be pronounced the divinest of men."

There is extant a collection of the sayings and doings of Confucius, as recorded by his disciples, which may be compared with portions of the four Gospels, inasmuch as we here find illustrated, sometimes vividly, the chief points of interest in his daily life and teaching; and it is from this source (the *Lun Yü*) that some of the quotations to follow have been taken.

Confucius is usually regarded as a teacher of morals only, and it is considered wrong, therefore, to class his doctrines as a religion. This is no doubt true, in the sense that he laid stress almost entirely upon man's duty to his neighbour, thinking, perhaps without going so very far astray, that the liver of a blameless life would not be far from the kingdom of God. But it is certain that he believed firmly in a higher Power—the God of his fathers, of whom we have already heard so much, and who, so far as we can deduce from the ancient records, was satisfied with right-doing on the part of mankind in reference to one another, and in other ways was less exacting than the "jealous God" of the Old Testament. Not only did Confucius, as we shall shortly see, believe in the existence of this Deity, more vaguely perhaps than did the anthropomorphic worshippers of early times; but he was conscious, and expressed his consciousness openly, that in his teachings he was working under divine guidance. Thus when, on his wanderings, he found himself in danger of violence, and his disciples were afraid, he reassured them, saying, "King Wên (see *ante*) being dead, has not his message been confided to me? If God had wished to put an end to this message, then I, King Wên's successor, should never have received it; but as God has not yet put an end to this message, what harm can these people do to me?" In another and similar case of danger, Confucius said, "God implanted the virtue that is in me; what can this man do to me?" Again, in reply to a disciple who asked what he meant by declaring, as just mentioned, that nobody knew him, Confucius said, "I do not murmur against God, nor do I grumble against man. My studies lie low, but they reach high; and there is God—He knows me. If my doctrines are to prevail, it is so ordered of God; if they are to fail, it is so ordered of God."

Nor was it only Confucius himself who held this view as to the divine character of his mission. After throwing up high office in his own native State of Lu, because his prince had accepted a present of eighty (one writer says only six) beautiful dancing-girls and was neglecting the administration of affairs, Confucius in a dejected mood set out on his travels. On arriving at the frontier of the Wei State, the warden in charge of the gate expressed a wish to meet the renowned sage, urging that when men of mark passed that way he was never denied the privilege of seeing them. He was accordingly introduced by the disciples; and when he came out he said, "My friends, why are you distressed by your Master's loss of office? The world has long been without right doctrines; now God is going to use him as a bell."

On a different plane, but still suggestive of something unusual in the personality of Confucius, is the following anecdote. Travelling along in a carriage, with a disciple in attendance, he came to a river, and sent the disciple to a couple of men working in the fields, in order to inquire for the ford. One of the men asked the disciple, "Who is that sitting in the carriage and holding the reins?" "It is Confucius," answered the disciple. "What! Confucius of the Lu State?" "Yes," replied the disciple. "Ah," said the man, speaking figuratively, "he knows the ford."

We must now see how far it is possible, using only genuine and not apocryphal utterances, to establish more conclusively the fact that Confucius fully recognized the existence of a Supreme Being. This recognition was indeed qualified by the maxim, already quoted, which he laid down for the guidance of others, namely, "Hear much, and put aside the points of which you are in doubt, while you also speak cautiously on the rest"; for there were four special subjects on which he himself would not willingly talk—uncanny manifestations, feats of strength, rebellion, and spiritual beings. But although he would not discuss in a familiar way the pros and cons of belief in an unseen world, probably because of the solemnity of the subject, he did not hesitate to use the name of the Deity in any suitable connexion. He does so when tracing the stages of his own career:

> At fifteen, my mind was bent on learning.
> At thirty, I stood firm.
> At forty, I had no doubts.
> At fifty, I knew the will of God.
> At sixty, I could trust my ears.
> At seventy, I could follow my heart's desires, without transgression.

A disciple being stricken with leprosy, Confucius went to inquire after him. He did not go into the house, but grasped the sick man's hand through the window, saying, "Alas! it is the will of God."

What was that which Confucius describes as the will of God, about which we are told in one passage that he did not care to speak? The word *ming*, here rendered by "will," or "command," also means "fate, destiny"; and there would be a serious claim for some such translation as "necessity" (Gr. ἀνάγκη), if ming were always found, as it is sometimes found, used alone, without the prefix of "God" (*T'ien ming*). The "necessity" of Greek philosophers has been defined as "a constraint conceived as a law prevailing throughout the material universe and within the sphere of human action"; it is never associated with any lawgiver, but proceeds from the natural constitution of things. It is quite clear, however, that whenever ming stands by itself in the ancient classical literature of China, it is elliptical for *T'ien ming*, the will, or decree, of God understood; just as, with us, the Word stands for Christ, the Messiah, known to the Jews as the Word of God.

There is one example which seems, but only seems, to militate against the above conclusion. A disciple mentions the following saying, which he states that he has heard, as some conjecture, from the lips of Confucius: "Life and death have their *ming*; riches and honours are in the hands of God." Now the first sentence looks as though it were "Life and death are matters of destiny"; that is, that they are events predetermined by the mysterious power or agency, not God, which we call Destiny or Fate. But here allowance must be made for the peculiarities of Chinese style, in which repetition is a common feature; not to mention that such a distribution of functions is quite out of the question—that is, the power of life and death being given to an abstraction, the disposition of such comparative trifles as wealth and honours to God. Therefore here, too, *ming* must stand for the will of God.

We will now pass on to the other frequent instances of the use by Confucius of the term "God," the Chinese equivalent being in every case *T'ien*, and not *Shang Ti*. Confucius went to pay a visit to a lady whose moral character did not stand high in public estimation. A disciple ventured to remonstrate with him for having done so; whereupon Confucius cried out with an oath, "If I have done anything wrong, may God strike me dead, may God strike me dead!"

The Golden Age of China, with its perfectly virtuous, semi-divine rulers, threw a lasting spell over the imagination of Confucius. It may partly have been a case of distance lending enchantment, for some of the great

Emperors of antiquity lived as long before his date as Confucius himself lived before ours; to us they are dimly seen, legendary beings, but to him they were moving, sentient heroes, drawing inspiration from on high. "Great indeed," he exclaims, "as a ruler, was the Emperor Yao; how majestic was he!" Then, in an afterthought, comes the reverential corrective: "It is only God who is really great: Yao took Him as his model."

Confucius being very ill, one of the disciples, named Yu, wished his colleagues to pretend to be officials in attendance, in order to create a similitude of the state to which the Master had been accustomed in the days when he held high office. But all Yu got for his trouble was to be rated, so soon as Confucius could speak, as an arrant hypocrite. " By pretending to have an official retinue," said Confucius, "when I have no such thing, upon whom should I impose? Should I impose upon God?"

Confucius had one favourite disciple, named Hui, who leaned upon him more than any of the others, and was never at any time a doubter or questioner of his Master's wisdom and divine mission. Of him Confucius said that for three months there would be nothing in his mind contrary to perfect virtue; that with a coarse platter of food, a gourd to drink out of, and a slum to live in—which would mean wretchedness to others—Hui would still be contented and happy; that he never let the sun go down upon his wrath (*cf.* Ephesians iv. 26); and was never twice guilty of the same lapse in conduct. But Hui died young, and in his grief Confucius cried out, "God is destroying me! God is destroying me!" At this the disciples who were with him remonstrated, saying, "Master, your grief is excessive." "My grief excessive?" cried Confucius. "If I am not to mourn bitterly for this man, for whom should I mourn?"

"There are three things," said Confucius, of which the superior man stands in awe. He stands in awe of the will of God. He stands in awe of great sages, and of the inspired words which have been uttered by such men." It was the dream of Confucius that all mankind should be composed of superior men, which makes it difficult for us to believe that he himself was, as he has been called too often, a mere moral philosopher, a materialist of the most pronounced type.

One more example of *T'ien* as understood by Confucius. He was protesting against the value of words as compared with deeds, and was applying the rule to his own individual case, when a disciple objected, saying, "If you,

Master, do not speak, what shall we, your disciples, have to record?" Confucius said, "Does God speak? The four seasons pursue their courses, and all things are regularly produced; but does God say anything?"

We will now transfer our attention more closely to the "spirits," which, as we have already seen, play such an important part in the earlier books of the Confucian Canon. From the sources available, it seems impossible to decide whether the recognition of a Supreme Being preceded or followed the belief that the souls of human beings enjoy continued existence after death. In regard to the relative importance of serving God and serving man, Confucius has often been blamed for setting man before God; but it should always be remembered that his interpretation of true service to God was embodied in right and proper performance of duty to one's neighbour. The idea of personal service to God Himself, as understood by the Jewish patriarchs, is entirely foreign to the Chinese conception of a Supreme Being.

Thus, when asked what constituted wisdom, Confucius replied, "To cultivate earnestly our duty towards our neighbour, and to reverence spiritual beings while maintaining always a due reserve, [1] may be called wisdom."

Again, when a disciple applied for guidance in serving the spirits of the dead, Confucius said, "Until you are able to serve men, how can you expect to serve their spirits?" The same questioner would have heard the Master's views on death; but Confucius said, "Until you understand life, how can you possibly understand death?"

We have, however, some interesting remarks on the supernatural world, which Confucius himself volunteered, without any pressure from an inquirer. "How abundantly," he said, "do spiritual beings make their presence manifest among us! We look for them, but do not see them; we listen for them, but do not hear them; yet they enter into all things, and there is nowhere where they are not. They cause all the people in the world to fast, and to put on their best clothes, in order to take part in the sacrifices. Then they seem to pass in waves, now over the heads, now at the very sides of the worshippers." In support of this, Confucius here

---

[1] Dr Legge has "to keep aloof from them," which would be equivalent to "have nothing to do with them." Confucius seems rather to have meant "no familiarity."

quotes three lines from the Odes, his hearers being, of course, able to supply the context from memory. They are taken from an ode which was written about the close of the ninth century B.C., by one of the feudal princes, and which was, quaintly enough, addressed to himself, as a means of keeping before his eyes the right conduct expected from one in his high station. Some of the lines which lead to the quotation used by Confucius run as follows:

> Shall not those of whom Almighty God does not approve,
> Surely as water flows down from a spring,
> Sink down together to ruin?
> Rise early and go to bed late;
> Sprinkle and sweep your courtyard,
> So as to be a pattern to your people.
> Have in good order your chariots and horses,
> Your bows and arrows, your weapons of war,
> So as to be prepared for warlike action.
> Be cautious in what you say;
> Be careful in what you do.
> A flaw in a piece of white jade
> May be ground away;
> But for a flaw in speech
> Nothing can be done.
> As seen in your friendship with good men,
> Your expression is conciliatory and kindly;
> You are anxious to do no wrong.
> As seen in your private chamber,
> You should also be free from shame.
> Do not say, "This place is not public;
> No one can see me here."

And now come the three lines quoted by Confucius:

> The advent of spiritual beings
> Cannot be known beforehand;
> All the less, then, should they be slighted.

If Confucius cannot be held to have spoken freely on the topic of spirits, at any rate he expanded somewhat in reference to the sacrifices of which spirits were the immediate object. We are told that he sacrificed to his dead ancestors as though those ancestors were present, and to spirits in general as though the spirits were present. He would not allow himself to be represented by proxy. "I regard," he said, "my absence from the ceremony as though I did not sacrifice." At the great sacrifice to the founder of the dynasty, which must have been a particularly solemn ceremony, Confucius said that after the pouring of the libation he had no wish to look on. It was at that moment, when the imagination of fervent worshippers was most powerfully stimulated, that the surrounding atmosphere, laden with the fumes of incense, seemed to be peopled, as it were, with spirits whose presence, if not seen, was unmistakably felt. From this atmosphere Confucius, for reasons which have not come down to us, wished to withdraw. Someone having asked him what was the meaning of the great sacrifice, Confucius replied, "I do not know. The man who knew its meaning would find it as easy to govern the empire as to look upon the palm of his hand." After what has been already quoted from his remarks on the influence of a spirit-world, it is impossible that he can have been actuated, in his wish not to look on, by unbelief. Perhaps he was overwhelmed by that same reverential feeling which prevented him from speaking on death and cognate subjects; that must remain for ever a matter of speculation. But just as it is obvious that Confucius believed in a God, so it is also obvious that he believed in the existence, and, on occasions, in the presence of spirits of the departed dead.

To go back a little, chronologically. The ruler of a certain feudal State, after petitioning God and receiving His sanction, determined (B.C. 648) for political reasons to hand over his territory to another State, and was explaining to a friend that the State about to absorb his own would keep up the proper sacrifices to his spirit after death. The friend remonstrated with him, saying, "I have heard that the spirits of the dead do not enjoy the sacrifices of those who are not of their kindred, and that people only sacrifice to those who are of the same ancestry as themselves. Will not, then, the sacrifices to your spirit be thus brought to an abrupt end?" This argument prevailed, and the principle enunciated was accepted and emphasized by Confucius, who declared that "for a man to sacrifice to a spirit which does not belong to him is flattery," and not legitimate worship. Temptations, however, are sometimes too strong for weak mortals. A Chinese merchant was discovered, not long ago, worshipping, with all the paraphernalia of eatables, wine, and paper money, at the grave of a recently deceased foreigner, his partner in trade; and he explained in pidgin-English that the dead man was an old friend, and that he hoped by the performance of this "joss-pidgin" to enlist the aid of his spirit in business transactions to come.

Among casual allusions by Confucius to sacrificial ceremonies, one or two are of more than passing interest. We are told that "when a friend sent him a present, though it might be a carriage and horses, he did not bow." The only present for which he bowed was that of flesh which had been used in sacrifice, and so consecrated by its dedication to the ancestral spirits of the giver. If his prince sent him a gift of cooked meat, he would straighten his mat before sitting down, and be the first to taste it. If the gift was raw flesh, he would have it cooked, and then offer it in sacrifice to the spirits of his own ancestors. The rule was that the oxen used at the great sacrifice should be red, and have good horns, qualifications which depended, we may take it, upon the pedigree of the animal. Thus, in reference to one of his most ardent disciples, who was the son of a bad father, Confucius pleaded as follows: "If the calf of a brindled cow be itself red and well horned, although men may not wish to use it, would the spirits of mountains and rivers put it aside?" The sins of the fathers were not to be visited upon the children.

It was customary in ancient China for the Emperor, at the end of each year, to distribute among the princes calendars showing the first day of each moon in the ensuing year. These were kept in the ancestral temple of the State; and on the first of every one of the following twelve moons they were brought out and the day was proclaimed, suggesting a comparison with the Latin word *Kalendae*, which meant the day when the order of days was proclaimed. To the ceremony of proclamation was attached the sacrifice of a sheep; and as the ceremony was beginning to be laxly observed, a disciple recommended that the sacrifice should be done away with. "My son," said Confucius, "you grudge the sheep; I grudge the sacrifice."

Confucius, when staying in the Wei State, was consulted by its ruler as to a military expedition which was about to be undertaken. He replied, "Matters which are concerned with sacrificial ceremonies are those with which I am familiar; as to military affairs, I know nothing about them." He then ordered his chariot and promptly quitted a territory where the arts of peace were to be subordinated to the art of war. "A bird," he exclaimed, "chooses the tree upon which it will roost; the tree does not choose the bird."

In the intimate conversations of Confucius with his disciples we do not come across any direct reference to divination; but from an essay composed by his grandson and disciple we learn that the reeds and the tortoise-shell were still employed, as we have already seen. We find allusions to fasting, which is mentioned, together with war and sickness, as one of three topics in regard to which Confucius exercised the greatest caution. We are told that "when fasting, he made a point of wearing clean clothes, always of linen cloth; he did not eat the same food as usual, nor would he sit in his accustomed place." It appears that fasting and purification were practised for about ten days before the performance of the sacrifices took place, but few reliable details of these rites have been handed down to us.

A word or two as to prayer, and its importance in the eyes of Confucius. Someone took occasion to ask him what was the interpretation of a vulgar proverb, which may be paraphrased as follows: "It is better to make friends with the kitchen than with the parlour," in allusion to the prayers and sacrifices offered to the spirit of the kitchen, and the greater likelihood of obtaining profit in that direction than from the more dignified spirit of the parlour. There was a political background to the question, which is of no consequence at the moment; all that we need trouble about is the answer. Confucius swept these petty rites aside, with the insignificant spirits, whom he evidently did not hold in the highest esteem, and, falling back on an older and loftier conception of man's guidance, replied, "He who has offended against God has none to whom he can pray."

Confucius being at another time very ill, a disciple asked leave to pray for him. "Is that usual?" he inquired. "It is," replied the disciple. "The Book of Prayer says, 'Pray to the spirits in heaven above and earth below.'" "In that case," said Confucius, "I have already been praying for a long time."

The question of mourning, as a rite, received some attention from Confucius. "Just as in festive ceremonies," he said, "it is better to be sparing than extravagant, so in mourning ceremonies it is better to be sincere than punctilious." Again: "Authority without mercy, ceremonial without reverence, mourning without sorrow—what have I to do with these?" His general attitude towards mourning and mourners was one of awe at finding himself in proximity to death and the unknown. We have it on record that "when the Master was eating by the side of a mourner, he never ate to repletion." Also: "When the Master saw a person in mourning garb, or a blind man, even though they were younger than himself, he would rise up; and if he had to pass them by, he would do so hastily." It was this same reverential feeling, and not fear, which caused him to turn pale at a clap of thunder, or in the presence of a hurricane. At that early date the thunderbolt was not regarded as one of the means at the disposal of the Almighty for punishing the derelictions of erring mortals. Time and superstition have succeeded in developing the modern god of thunder who, accompanied by a goddess, goes about dealing destruction to the wicked. The goddess holds in her hand a bright mirror, with which she flashes a ray of lightning on to the doomed man, so that the god of thunder may see where to launch his bolt.

It has always been the rule in China to wear mourning for parents, nominally for a space of three years, actually for twenty-seven months. Attempts to shorten this trying period have been made, but without success. An Emperor of the second century B.C. asked with his dying breath that the people might not be forced to observe the very inconvenient ceremonies of national mourning prescribed upon a demise of the throne, but be allowed to marry and give in marriage as usual, thus not wasting too much energy on such an unworthy creature as himself. Only those who have witnessed a national mourning under the Manchus can have any idea of the hardships entailed on the masses by the death of an Emperor, although the length of time imposed by regulation was nothing like three years in duration. Still, for a hundred days no one might have his head shaved; and the barbers, but for the patriarchal system, would have starved. No marriages could be solemnized within a year; and during the same period large troupes of actors were thrown out of employ, for all theatres were closed. Festivities and music were altogether prohibited. On the death of a parent, an official was compelled, except for a special dispensation from the Emperor, to go into retirement for the full term of twenty-seven months.

A disciple asked Confucius about the three years' mourning for parents, saying that one year was surely long enough. "If the superior man," he argued, "abstains for three years from ceremonial observances, those observances will be quite lost. If for three years he abstains from music, there will be an end to music. Every year we have new grain taking the place of the old grain which is exhausted, and once every year (a ceremony at the winter solstice) we produce a fresh supply of fire. One year, therefore, should be enough." On this Confucius said, "If, after only a year's mourning, you were to eat good food and wear embroidered clothes, would you feel happy?" "I should," replied the disciple. "Well then," said Confucius, "if you can feel happy, do it. But a superior man, while in mourning, will not enjoy dainty food, nor take pleasure in music, nor even rest in comfort; therefore he does not do it. Your case is different." When the disciple had withdrawn, Confucius said, "He is lacking in right feeling. It is not until a child is three years old that it can do without the arms of its parents; therefore the three years' period of mourning is universally observed throughout the empire."

A Confucian dogma, often attributed to Confucius, and also with more reason to Mencius, who, as we shall see, was its chief exponent, asserts that all men are born good. This is in direct antagonism to that Christian dogma which is based upon the fall of man as related in the book of Genesis, and teaches that the imagination of man's heart is evil from his youth (ch. viii. 21). The germ, however, of the Chinese view is much older than Confucius. It is found in the Odes; and the utmost we can really claim is that Confucius accepted any and all of the doctrines in the work which passed through his hands as editor. For he once said to his disciples, "My children, why do you not study the Odes? They stimulate the mind. They teach observation. They warn against hatred. From them you learn, at home, to serve your father, abroad, to serve your prince; from them you can also learn the names of many birds, beasts, and plants." He one day asked his son, "Have you learnt the Odes?" and on receiving the answer, "Not yet," proceeded to say that until the young man had done so, he would not be fit for polite society. On another occasion he said, "The Odes consist of three hundred poems, and the gist of them all may be summed up in a word: Have no impure thoughts." We therefore seem to be justified in concluding that Confucius accepted the dogma, "Man is born good." The particular verse in the Odes which bears out the statement that Confucius was not the originator of the dogma in question, runs as follows:

> How great is God,
> The ruler of men below!
> How arrayed in terrors is God!
> Yet His will is often disregarded.
> God created the myriad people,
> Yet His ordinances are not relied upon.
> All men are good at birth,
> But not many remain so to the end.

It is probable that few tasks will be found so impracticable as the effort to wean the Chinese people, soaked, so to speak, in the authority of centuries, from this belief in the natural goodness of mankind, to another belief, in exactly opposite terms, which peoples this world with successive generations of little children born in sin. [1]

This doctrine of original purity, coupled with the practice of ancestral worship, together form an important cleavage, not easy to be bridged over, between Christianity and Confucianism. Points of contact, however, between these two religions, if I may now be allowed to apply this term equally to both, are many and striking. The two following examples can scarcely be ignored. (1) When asked by a disciple for a rule of life, Confucius replied, "Do not unto others what you would not they should do unto you." Attempts have been made to minimize the value of this maxim, which is, of course, identical with that enunciated by Christ and known as the Golden Rule, on the ground that it is in a negative form, and therefore not of such direct force. But the fallacy of this position may be shown in a few words. What you would not wish men to do to you, would be to abstain from helping you when in trouble. Do not therefore abstain from helping others when they are in trouble; in other words, do help them. (2) Another disciple having asked for an explanation of the Chinese term for "charity of heart" (*cf.* 1 Cor. xiii.), Confucius replied, "Love one another!"

The more practical character of Confucianism as contrasted with Christianity is abundantly manifest. Confucius was entirely in sympathy with human weaknesses, and did not put man's faith to too severe a test. He would have echoed such sentiments as "He that is without sin among you, let him first cast a stone"; but such poetical commands as to turn the other cheek to the smiter, or to give up your cloke to the enemy who has just succeeded in obtaining your coat, would find no place in his teachings. On the other hand, his concessions to humanity may be regarded by some as stretching the gift of charity of heart to breaking point. For instance, he declared that a man who should be without reproach in regard to the main principles of human conduct, might fairly be excused any lapses in regard to smaller issues, which seems to traverse Christ's declaration, "He that is unjust in the least is unjust also in much." Again, one of the feudal princes

---

[1] "Original sin, with which all mankind, descended from fallen Adam by natural generation, are universally infected from their conception and birth." Parkhurst on Romans v. 12.

was boasting to Confucius of the high level of morality which prevailed in his own State. "Among us here," he said, "you will find upright men. If a father has stolen a sheep, his son will give evidence against him." "In my part of the country," replied Confucius, there is a different standard from this. A father will shield his son, and a son will shield his father. It is thus that uprightness will be found."

There is in Chinese a word which is used of Confucius and of three or four of the other great men of remote antiquity, such as the Emperors Yao and Shun. It signifies a human being who, by the grace of God, is divinely good and intuitively wise, and therefore an infallible exponent of right and wrong. Our nearest English equivalent is perhaps "inspired." Confucius himself discusses the term (*Chung Yung*, xx.) as follows: "Truth is that which God is, and man attains to. He who is an embodiment of truth hits his mark without taking aim, apprehends without thought, and naturally and easily strikes the right path. Such a man is inspired." Confucius disclaimed any right to this exalted title, although, as we have seen, he did at times regard himself as an instrument of the Almighty. He says in one passage (*Lun Yü*, vii.), "As for the inspired man and the man of perfect charity of heart, how dare I rank myself with them? It may simply be said of me, that I strive to become such without satiety, and to teach others without weariness." What his disciples thought of their Master may be gathered from a few extracts which they have left behind them. A spiteful man having said that a certain one of the disciples was greater than Confucius, on the remark coming to his ears, that disciple said, "Let us think in terms of houses with walls round them. My wall reaches only to the shoulders. You can peep over it and see the pleasant arrangement within. Now, my Master's wall is many feet in height; and unless you go in by the door, you cannot see the ancestral temple with all its beauties and the various officers in rich array. But few are those," he added, "who find that door."

One more testimonial from a similar source (*Chung Yung*, xxxi.). "All-embracing and vast, Confucius is like the sky. Deep-centred, he is like the abyss. He appears, and the people all revere him; he speaks, and the people all believe him. Therefore his fame overspreads the Middle Kingdom, and extends to the barbarous tribes. Wherever ships and carriages reach; wherever the strength of man penetrates; wherever the sky covers and the earth supports; wherever the sun and moon shine;

wherever frosts and dews fall—all who have blood and breath unfeignedly love and honour him. Hence it is said, He is the peer of God."

After the death of the Master, the torch of Confucianism was handed on chiefly by his grandson and disciple, K'ung Chi, whose famous essay, known as the Doctrine of the Mean (*Chung Yung*), has been already quoted. With this essay, which traces the ruling motives of human conduct to a psychological source, we are not now concerned. It contains, however, a couplet from the Odes, with the writer's own exegesis, which may perhaps be worth recording.

> The will of God is manifested
> In wondrous and ceaseless ways!

This means, says K'ung Chi, that "what God does, that is God"—a remarkable statement with which may be compared Aristotle's conception of God as ἐνέργεια, existence in action, or *actus purus*. [1]

While fully recognizing the sincerity and value of the efforts of the earlier disciples to keep alight what was to them the sacred flame of Confucianism, it must be freely admitted that the firm hold which these doctrines took upon the imagination of the Chinese people, and which has been maintained with extraordinary persistence through some twenty-three centuries past, would never have been brought about but for the genius and labours of Mencius, who now enjoys the title of the Second Inspired One, bestowed upon him in A.D. 1330. Born almost exactly a century after the death of Confucius, he devoted his life to the glorification of Confucianism; and if he ventured to lead his hearers into new lines of thought, the foundations on which these lines rested were always to be found in the bed-rock laid by his Master. Confucius, as we have seen, dealt principally with lofty moral precepts and their practical application to everyday life. Mencius went further afield and handled political and economical problems with the object of securing national right conduct through the medium of national prosperity. No one pretends that he reached the high level on which Confucianism was established; but he is honoured for what he did towards consolidating that establishment, by teaching and preaching throughout his life its supremacy over all other forms of doctrine. He might indeed be regarded as the St Paul of Confucianism, were it not that

---

[1] Kindly suggested by Prof. James Ward.

he handed on the creed of the Founder in all its native simplicity and beauty, without addition or garnish of any kind. There is no such thing as Mencian Confucianism, to correspond to Pauline Christianity.

Let us see what Mencius has to say about God, omitting those references which are merely quotations from the Odes or the Canon of History. One of the feudal princes consulted him as to the best method of dealing with neighbouring States, so as to ensure the continuance of friendly intercourse. Mencius replied that if it was a case of furthering the interests of a less powerful State, then perfect charity of heart would be necessary to the ruler of the more powerful State, in order to secure the proper treatment of his weaker neighbour. On the other hand, if it was a case of furthering the interests of a more powerful State, then perfect wisdom would be necessary to the ruler of the less powerful State, in order to achieve a satisfactory result. "For the ruler of a powerful State," said Mencius, "who furthers the interests of a weaker State, is one who loves God (*T'ien*); and the ruler of a weak State who furthers the interests of a more powerful State, is one who fears God. He who loves God will be a protector of the whole empire; he who fears God will protect his own State."

Allusions to the will of God are frequent. The capture of a city, or the continuance of a princely line are alike dependent upon the will of God. Calamities and blessings are traced to the same source. "When the empire is well governed," says Mencius, "right prevails, and good men triumph over the wicked; when it is badly governed, might prevails, and the strong triumph over the weak. Such are the dispensations of God; but those who obey God are saved, while those who disobey perish."

In one instance, Mencius quotes a statesman (I Yin) who flourished in the eighteenth century before Christ, and who is reported to have said, "When God created mankind, His plan was that those who possessed intuitive wisdom should enlighten those who were capable only of acquiring wisdom; and that those who possessed intuitive enlightenment should enlighten those who were capable only of acquiring enlightenment." This must mean that God conveyed His will by means of chosen vessels, that is, inspired men, or prophets.

Mencius held that all earthly honours came not from man, but from God. The prince was the apparent source, but really only the agent of the Almighty, entrusted with the task of discovering and rewarding virtuous men. Borrowing examples from antiquity, such as Shun, the ploughman-Emperor, he further shows that "when God is about to confer a great office on any man, He first chastens that man's mind with suffering, and his sinews and bones with toil. He exposes that man's body to hunger, and subjects him to extreme poverty. He confounds that man's undertakings; and by these methods stimulates his mind, softens his nature, and supplies his deficiencies." Just so we read in Revelation iii. 19, "As many as I love, I rebuke and chasten."

"Everything depends," says Mencius, "upon the will of God; therefore a man should accept submissively whatever can properly be ascribed thereto (*ut melius quicquid erit pati*). He who understands what is meant by the will of God will not place himself under a tottering wall. Death in the discharge of one's duties may properly be ascribed to the will of God; but death in gyves and fetters cannot be so ascribed."

Still upholding the belief in an anthropomorphic God, as described in our first lecture, Mencius taught that man was created in God's own image. "Our physical bodies," he said, "in regard to shape and appearance, are of the nature of God; but a man must be divinely inspired before he can adequately sustain that nature." Man's mental and moral qualifications, too, did not, according to Mencius, reach him by chance, but were specially conferred. Confucius had said that in choosing a dwelling-place, a wise man would be chiefly attracted by the prevalence of a charitable spirit among those who would be his immediate neighbours. On this, Mencius comments: "Charity of heart is the noblest gift of God; it is a house, so to speak, in which a man may live in peace. No one can prevent us from possessing this gift; if we have it not, that is due to our own folly." Again, Mencius says, "There are dignities of God, and there are dignities of man. Charity of heart, duty towards one's neighbour, loyalty, and truth—these are the dignities of God. To be a duke, a minister of State, or a high official—these are the dignities of man. The men of old cultivated the dignities of God, and the dignities of man followed. The men of to-day cultivate the dignities of God in order to secure the dignities of man; and when they have obtained the dignities of man, they cast aside all further thought of the dignities of God. In this they greatly err, and the probability is that they will lose their dignities of man as well." Referring again to charity of heart, the first and most powerful of all the Confucian virtues, Mencius gives an interesting similitude. "Charity of heart," he says, "subdues uncharitableness just as water subdues fire. But people nowadays employ charity of heart much in the same way as if they were to try to put out a blazing cartload of firewood with a single cupful of water; and then when they fail to put out the flames, they turn round and blame the water."

The term used for God by Mencius is *T'ien*; there is only one instance of his use of the alternative *Shang Ti*. It occurs in the following rather curious sentence: "If a great beauty were to appear in a foul and filthy head-dress, people would all hold their noses when passing her. If a leper were to fast, abstain from wine, and purify himself by a bath, he might be allowed to sacrifice to God." In every other case we find *T'ien*, the term which supplies the anthropomorphic figure of the Supreme Being. Thus, we have *T'ien* when Mencius declares it to be one of the joys of the superior man, that looking up, he has no occasion for shame before God, and looking down, he has no occasion to blush before men."

We have seen that the belief in the existence of spirits finds its first expression in the worship of ancestors. In the presence of death, primeval man in China must have sought for some explanation of the body, just now full of life and movement, then, suddenly, an inert mass. Aided by dreams, in which the dead so often reappear, he must gradually have come to regard the body as matter informed by a vital essence, the separation of which produced the phenomenon of death. As time went on, a spirituality associated with thunder, wind, rain, rivers, trees, and mountains, gradually crystallized into beings susceptible of propitiation and able to confer benefits upon mankind.

"Wherever the superior man passes," says Mencius, "he civilizes; and he leaves behind him an atmosphere of spirituality;" that is, an influence of a divine character, with a tendency to spread far and wide. In another passage we come almost into touch with the unseen. After showing the steps which lead up to real goodness, Mencius says, "A great and good man who exercises a civilizing influence is called an inspired man. An inspired man whose personality transcends our knowledge is a spirit." It is difficult to say precisely what this last sentence means; the reference is apparently to a class of celestial beings, inferior to the Deity, but possessed of supernatural power; approximately, angels.

Among those spirits whose development seems to have followed most closely upon the recognition by the people at large of a Supreme Being, must be mentioned the tutelary spirits of the land and of grain. In this connexion, there is a remarkable statement by Mencius, illustrating a well-known attitude of primitive peoples towards their gods or fetishes, which are so often discarded when found to be inefficient. "The people," said Mencius, "are of the first importance; the spirits of the land and grain come next; the sovereign is of less account. If a prince abuses his position in regard to the spirits of the land and grain (that is, if he is a bad ruler), he is deposed and another is put in his place. On the other hand, if the sacrificial victims have been perfect, the sacrificial grain clean, and the sacrifices offered at the proper season;—then, if a drought should follow, or a flood, the spirits of the land and grain would be deposed and others put in their places."

No utterances of Mencius are of more importance, or have been cherished with more reverence, than those arguments by which he supported and finally established the Confucian dogma that the nature of man at his birth is pure and free from evil. These arguments, together with those of his opponents, I propose to submit in my next lecture. There is, however, one statement on man's nature with which I will now conclude. Mencius said, "He who brings all his intellect to bear on the subject, will come to understand his own nature; he who understands his own nature will understand God. To preserve one's intellect, and to nourish one's nature—that is how to serve God. To waste no thoughts upon length of life, but to cultivate rectitude—that is to do the will of God." Confucianism has often been stigmatized as a mere philosophy, inadequate to the spiritual needs of man; the last words, however, of the above quotation go far to show that the cultivation of rectitude is, according to Confucian teachings, broad based upon the will of God.

B.C. 300-200

WE now come to the arguments by which Mencius sought to prove that the original nature of man is good, and becomes corrupted only by environment. A philosopher of the day, named Kao, said, "Man's nature may be likened to a willow-tree, and duty towards one's neighbour to a bowl. You get charity of heart and duty towards one's neighbour out of man's nature just as you get a wooden bowl out of a willow-tree." "Sir," replied Mencius, "Can you get bowls from willow-trees without injuring the original nature of the trees? In order to get your bowl, you must first kill and rob the tree; and by parity of reasoning, in order to get charity of heart and duty towards one's neigh-bour, you must first kill and rob the man. The result would be that all mankind would regard charity of heart and duty towards one's neighbour as nothing better than calamities."

The philosopher Kao said, "Man's nature is like rushing water; make a passage for it towards the east, and it will flow eastwards; make a passage for it towards the west, and it will flow westward. Man's nature has no particular bent towards good or evil, any more than water has a particular bent towards east or west." "Water has indeed no bias," replied Mencius, "either east or west; but will it flow indifferently up or down? Man's bent towards good may be likened to the tendency of water to flow downwards. There are no men but have this bent towards good, just as there is no water which does not flow downwards. Of course, by striking it, you can make water jump up over your head, and you can also, by proper management, force it up a hill (as by water-wheels); but is this in accordance with the nature of water? It is simply a question of force; and if men are caused to do what is not good, it is in precisely the same way."

The philosopher Kao said, "What is reached at birth, that is the nature." "Do you mean to say, then," inquired Mencius, "that, in a similar way, all white is white?" "I do," replied Kao. "Do you mean," continued Mencius, "that the whiteness of a white feather is the same as the whiteness of snow, and that the whiteness of white snow is the same as the whiteness of white jade?" "I do," replied Kao. "Then," said Mencius, "you evidently mean that the nature of a dog is the same as that of an ox, and that the nature of an ox is the same as that of a man."

Wishing for more direct instructions than can be found in the above, a disciple said to Mencius, "There is the philosopher Kao; he declares that the nature of man is neither good nor bad. Others say that it may be trained to do either good or evil; others, again, say that some natures are good and some bad; and now you say that man's nature is good. Then are all those wrong?" "To judge by our feelings," replied Mencius, "man's nature is adapted for the practice of what is good; and that is what I mean when I say it is good. if a man does what is evil, the blame cannot be laid upon his natural powers." Mencius goes on to show that certain feelings, such as pity, shame, respect, and sense of right and wrong, belong to the four virtues, charity of heart, duty towards one's neighbour, propriety, and wisdom respectively, all of which, Mencius tells us, are certainly innate; but it is still more difficult to see how this advances the position. His language is clearer when he says, "In good years, the young men have the wherewithal to feed themselves, but in bad years they become desperate. This is not because God has given them different temperaments for different occasions, but because their minds sink under the strain of exceptional circumstances."

Mencius proceeds to argue that crops of barley, for instance, if sown under identical conditions, will yield identical results; and that if there are any differences in results between the harvests of two crops, this will be due to inequalities of soil, of rainfall, or of cultivation, and not to any difference in the nature of the barley. Why, then, should man form an exception to the rule? He quotes in support of this an old philosopher who said, "If a man were to make sandals without knowing the size required, I know that he would not make them as big as clothes-baskets," the reason given for this being that all sandals are alike and all feet much the same in size. Again, Mencius says, "If men differed in their taste for food in the same way that men differ in this respect from dogs and horses, how could there ever have arisen a standard cookery which is generally accepted? It must be, therefore, that men's palates are alike. And so with regard to music, and even beauty, for which there are fixed standards of taste; and this being the case, is it likely that men's minds can be without some common standard? Where, then, do we find this common standard? It is to be found in the eternal principles and practice of right and wrong. The inspired sages of old were merely beforehand in expressing feelings which I now share with all man- kind, and of which I approve in the same way that my palate approves of such food as is commonly approved of by all men."

"There is the Ox Mountain," said Mencius, "which was once overgrown with beautiful trees. The mountain, however, was situated on the frontier between two States; and in process of time all the trees were hacked about until there was very little left of them. Even when the trees did attempt to sprout again, cattle and goats came and browsed upon the young shoots, and the mountain was stripped bare, so that nowadays people do not understand that it was once finely wooded. But is bareness the nature of that mountain? And can we then say that the human mind is devoid of a sense of charity and duty? No; a man's moral sense suffers loss just as trees suffer under the axe. Day by day hacked about, how can they retain their beauty? Then comes the restoring influence of night, when the moral sense reasserts itself; still, the fetters and gyves of the day more than counteract this influence, and men sink to the level of brutes, in which condition it would seem that charity of heart and duty towards one's neighbour had never had any place in their minds. Can this condition be regarded as fitting for the human race? If it receive its proper nourishment, there is nothing that will not grow; if this nourishment is wanting, there is nothing which will not decay. Confucius said, 'Hold fast to your moral sense, and it will remain with you; let it go, and you will lose it.'"

It was thus that Mencius satisfied himself and others that Confucius was not in error when he handed down the tradition that man is born good; a dogma which has ever since been accepted by Confucianists as the keystone of their arch. Its validity was disputed some few years later by a philosopher, named Hsün (see *ante*), who wrote an essay to prove that the nature of man at birth is evil. "A crooked stick," says Hsün Tzŭ, "must be softened and bent, if you want to make it straight; a blunt knife must be applied to the grindstone, if you want to make it sharp; and the nature of man, being evil, must be submitted to teachers and laws, if you want to make it correct. Our nature is from God; it cannot be obtained by learning and striving. It is erroneous to say that the nature of man is originally good, and that it becomes bad by association and environment. If the nature of a man, with which he is born, can diverge from its original purity, that nature is gone; and this makes it clear that the nature must have been evil to start with. Indeed, if it were really good, it would need no training to keep it so. The nature of the eye is to see, and the nature of the ear is to hear; if man's nature could be regarded as something which was so at the beginning and remained so without assistance of any kind, then we might say that the nature of man is good, in the same way that we say the eyes see and the ears hear. If a man is good, that is an artificial result. For, his condition being what it is, he is influenced first of all by a desire for gain. Hence, he strives to get all he can without consideration for his neighbour. Secondly, he is liable to envy and hate. Hence, he seeks the ruin of others, and loyalty and truth are set aside. Thirdly, he is a slave to his animal passions. Hence, he commits excesses, and wanders from the path of duty and right. Thus, conformity with man's natural disposition leads to all kinds of violence, disorder, and ultimate barbarism. Only under the restraint of law and of lofty moral influences does man eventually become fit to be a member of regularly organized society. From these premises we must necessarily conclude that by nature man is evil; and that if he becomes good, that is an artificial result."

Apart from the question of man's nature at birth, Hsün Tzŭ has something to say on man's relations with the Deity. "God," he argues, "is consistent in His actions, but it is not He who preserves the good man and destroys the bad. A ruler who responds with good government is happy; whereas bad government leads to his destruction. If a man is thrifty and economical, then God cannot make him poor; if he takes care of himself at all seasons, then God cannot make him sick; if he is single-minded in his pursuit of what is right, then God cannot bring misfortune upon him. Therefore, floods and drought will not cause him to hunger and thirst; heat and cold will not be able to affect his health; nor will devils and bogies be able to destroy him. So, too, if a man is extravagant, God cannot make him rich; if he neglects his health, God cannot make him whole; and if he strays from the true path, God cannot make him happy. Before floods and drought can reach him, he will already hunger and thirst; before cold and heat can attack him, he will already be sick; and before devils and bogies can seize him, he will already be destroyed. For such calamities," continues Hsün Tzŭ, "God is not to be blamed; and whosoever can rightly apportion the respective shares of God and man in the scheme of the universe, such a one may be styled perfect indeed."

Hsün Tzŭ set his face against superstition. "When stars fall or trees shriek, all cry out in fear, 'What's that?' I say, "Tis nothing but some natural process which we may marvel at, not fear.'" Again—a favourite quotation—"God does not speak, yet the four seasons pursue their regular course; and just so, inspired men give spiritual guidance, and the whole world obeys them. God is truth, and He expresses it by their help. He does not speak, yet we trust Him; the spirits are not angry, yet we hold them in awe. The inscrutableness of God constitutes His divinity; the unchangeableness of this divinity constitutes God. God is immanent in all things; there is nowhere where He is not. God takes cognizance of objective existences, not by the senses of hearing and sight, nor by any working of the mind, but through that principle to which all physical things and all moral questions are subordinate, which is more effective than the senses or the workings of the mind. God sees and hears through the medium of the people, and is influenced accordingly; therefore it has been said that God is the expression of the people's hearts. The spirits of nature have their limitations, and cannot make themselves everywhere heard. The spirit recognized by the inspired man is God alone, who can penetrate and make Himself known through all things."

The Chinese people decided early not to allow the logic of Hsün Tzŭ to displace the already accepted arguments of Mencius. Luckily for himself, Mencius was no longer alive when the controversy broke out. He had had a sufficient task, as it was, in combating other doctrines. "Master," said a disciple to hire, "people all say that you are fond of disputing; I venture to ask if that is so." "It is not," replied Mencius; "the fact is that I cannot do otherwise." He then proceeds to give reasons. "Unemployed scholars," said Mencius, "are discussing unorthodox themes. The words of Yang Chu and Mo Ti fill the empire, and those who are not on the side of one will be found on the side of the other. Yang's doctrine is *Every man for himself*, which means that he recognizes no ruler. Mo's doctrine is *Love all equally*, which means that he does not recognize the special claim of a parent. But to recognize neither parent nor ruler is to be a brute beast. If these doctrines are not checked, and the doctrines of Confucius are not put forward, heterodox teachings will delude the people, and charity of heart and duty towards one's neighbour will cease to prevail. Then, beasts will be led on to devour men, and men will soon be devouring one another. I am alarmed by these things, and address myself to the doctrines of the inspired men of old in order to oppose Yang and Mo."

There is another passage where Mencius, alluding to the system of ethical egoism preached by Yang Chu, has the following words: "Though he might have benefited the whole world by plucking out a single hair, he would not have done it." This is not quite fair to Yang Chu. The story is that someone said to him, "If by plucking a single hair from your body you could save the whole world, would you do it?" "The world could not possibly be saved by a single hair," replied Yang. "But if it could be so saved," said his questioner, "would you do it?" To this Yang made no reply. For us, no reply is necessary; the mere fact of such a question being put to him is sufficient to disclose the general trend of his teachings. He was an uncompromising pessimist, and answered the famous question "is life worth living?" by an emphatic negative. He argued that even if a man lived to a hundred, so many years would have to be deducted for infancy, sleep, pain and sickness, anxiety and sorrow, and for the dotage of old age, that barely ten years would be left for not altogether unclouded enjoyment.

"What then," he asked, "can be the object of human existence? Wherein is happiness to be found?—In the appointments of wealth and luxury? In the enjoyment of the pleasures of sense? Alas! those will not always charm, and these may not always be enjoyed. Besides, there is the stimulus of good report, there is the restraint of law, in things we may do and in things we may not do. And thus we struggle on for a breath of fame, scheming to be remembered after death; ever on our guard against the allurements of sense, ever on the watch over our hearts and actions. We miss whatever of real happiness is to be got out of life, never being able for a single moment to relax the vigilance of our heed. In what, indeed, do we differ from the fettered captives of a gaol? The men of old knew that with life they had come but for a while, and that with death they would shortly depart. Therefore they followed the desires of their own hearts, and did not deny themselves pleasures to which they felt naturally inclined. Fame tempted them not; but led by their instincts alone, they took such enjoyments as lay in their path, not seeking for a name beyond the grave. They were thus out of the reach of censure; while as for precedence among men, or length or shortness of life, these gave them no concern whatever." To one who asked if speedy death would not be preferable to length of years, and suggested suicide, Yang Chu replied, "No; since you have got life, do not trouble about it, but simply bear it; enjoy yourself as best you can while waiting for death. When death is at hand, do not trouble about it, but simply face it; take that which comes, and yield yourself up to annihilation."

The philosopher Mo, who suffered at the hands of Mencius a castigation similar to that dealt out to Yang Chu, seems to have done no more than propound, as a remedy for all manner of existing evils, the simple doctrine above-mentioned—an equal love of one's fellow-creatures.

As a specimen of Mo Tzǔ's reasoning, we may take the following parable. There are two men, one of whom discriminates in his love for his fellows; the other, in accordance with the teaching of Mo Tzǔ, loves all men equally. The former argues, "I cannot feel for my friend so strongly as I feel for myself, neither can I feel for my friend's parents so strongly as I feel for my own parents." As a consequence of this, he may see his friend hungry, and will not feed him; he may see him cold, and will not clothe him; he may see him sick, and will not nurse him; he may see him dead, and will not bury him. The latter argues, "He who wishes to play a lofty part among men, will feel for his friend as he feels for himself, and for his friend's parents as for his own." Therefore, when he sees his friend hungry, he will feed him; cold, he will clothe him; sick, he will nurse him; and dead, he will bury him. Such will be the language of one who loves all men equally, and such will be his conduct. As a counsel of perfection, there is doubtless little to say against this; but Mencius was a Confucianist to the backbone, and jealous of what he fancied might involve even the faintest deviation from the way of his Master. Therefore Yang Chu and Mo Tzǔ had to go; and, in the striking words of a native critic, "Mencius snuffed them out."

Between 332 and 295 B.C. there lived one Ch'ü P'ing, a famous statesman and poet, whose name is still a household word in China. In despair at the unsatisfactory political outlook, he committed suicide by drowning; and the search for his body has ever since been commemorated at all important centres by an annual regatta, known as the Dragon Festival. His writings, which remain to us, contain many allusions to a Deity—*the* Deity, in fact, with whom we became so familiar in the Odes. "Man," he says, "sprang originally from God, just as the individual comes from his parents. When the span of man is at an end, he goes back to that from which he sprang. Thus it is that in the hour of bitter trial and exhaustion, there is no man but calls to God, just as in his hours of sickness and sorrow every one of us will turn to his parents."

Among his poems are some songs, written when in exile to replace the coarse ditties used at sacrifices to God. They were sung to an accompaniment of music and dancing, and a priest or augur seems to have acted as a medium between the worshippers and the Deity. One of the songs runs as follows:

> The day is propitious, and well-timed the hour;
> Let us begin to give pleasure to God.

> Let us grasp the hilts of our long swords,
> Let our jade ornaments tinkle and clang,
> Let us have jasper couches and jade ear-plugs.
> Why does not the augur seize the coral branch and diffuse fragrance?
> Let us cook the orchid to provide the food;
> Let us set forth offerings of cassia wine and pepper sauce;
> Let us raise the drumstick and strike the drums,
> At long intervals and slowly, with restrained song.
> Then arrange the pipes and the psaltery, and lift up your voices,
> And the medium will begin to dance in his grand vestments.
> Delicious perfumes fill the hall;
> The five notes [1] break into harmonious music,
> And God is happy and at peace.

The ear-plugs, mentioned above, are held by some to have been mere ornaments, hanging down from the cap in front of the ears; it seems, however, more reasonable to regard them as used for stopping up the ear, not after the fashion of Herbert Spencer to shut out conversation, but simply to keep out the dust. The coral branch, with which the augur or medium diffused fragrance, was a magical branch plucked from a coral tree in fairyland; in fact, a kind of Chinese

"golden bough." The slow time of the music was arranged to suit the slow movements of the dancer.

Another poem is addressed to "The Infinite One," whose presence is invoked on behalf of worshippers:

> Bathed in orchid water, washed with perfumes,
> Dressed in robes gay-coloured like the alpinia,
> The medium performs the ceremony of introducing the Spirit,
> Whose glory shines around, magnificent beyond conception.
> Ah, now it is at rest in our Hall of Longevity,
> Rivalling in brightness the sun and the moon!
> Now God, the Spirit, rides in His dragon chariot,
> And in His flight circles around hither and thither.
> When God has come down in all His glory,

---

[1] Of the ancient Chinese scale.

> He rapidly returns to His home in the distant sky.
> He casts His eye over central China and all around,
> Across the boundless spaces of the Four Seas. . . .
> Longing to be with Thee, I sigh deeply,
> And am overwhelmed in my heart with grief.

An attempt has been made by some Chinese critics to show that this poem is an allegory, and that the Deity with whom the writer longs to be at rest is his prince, who has fallen into evil hands and will not listen to his counsels. But it appears rather to be a general expression that he is fatigued with life, and not loth to part, his ever perfervid imagination being highly stimulated by the sacrificial ceremonies and consciousness of the divine presence. He devoted another and much longer poem, entitled "Sinking into Sadness," to chagrin at his ill-success with his prince, describing with an extraordinary wealth of imagery a flight from one end of the universe to the other, in search of Truth and Honour, first with a phœnix as his chariot, drawn by a dragon, and again in a jasper and ivory car to which flying dragons were harnessed. But all in vain; for he found himself back at his native place without having discovered the objects of his search.

Ch'ü P'ing passed on the traditional belief in a spiritual survival after death. At the end of a battle-piece he has the following lines:

> As evening fell, our ardour grew fiercer;
> Our best men were all killed; their bodies lay on the plain.
> They came out but did not go in, they went but did not return;
> The road home from the battle-field was too long.
> There they lay with their great swords, and grasping their bows;
> Heads were separated from bodies, yet hearts never quailed.
> Being thus brave, and soldiers to boot,
> Their vigorous resistance could not be broken.
> And now that their bodies are dead, their divine spirits
> Shall become leaders in the army of disembodied ghosts.

In the words of a modern patriotic song—

> Their souls go marching on.

One of his longer poems consists of a string of questions addressed direct to the Deity. It is strangely entitled "God Questions," and not, as we should expect, "Questions to God," because, as the Chinese editor tells us, "God is an object of reverence and cannot be questioned; therefore the words are transposed." The poem opens as follows:

> At the beginning of antiquity,
> Who was there to hand down the story?
> When heaven and earth were without form, p. 111
> Who examined and found them so?
> The mysterious sequence of light and darkness,
> Who could penetrate it?
> In the confusion of chaos,
> How could matter be recognized as such?
> The changes of light and darkness,
> How were they periodically brought about?
> The male and female principles, our progenitors,
> What was their origin, and how did they develop?
> The nine layers of the round sky,
> Who has measured them,
> And by whose skill were they constructed?
> How was the turning-rope attached,
> And how was the pole fixed?
> How do the Eight Mountains support the sky,
> And why is the south-east (towards which rivers flow) low lying?
> What do they rest on?
> The nooks and corners of the universe,
> Who can count them?
> Where is the sky joined to the earth,
> And who divided the twelve signs of the zodiac?
> How are the sun and the moon fastened on,
> And how are the constellations laid out?
> From its rising to its setting,
> How many miles does the sun travel?
> What virtue is there in the moon
> By which it dies and is born again?
> What does the hare expect to get
> By sitting gazing in the body of the moon?
> The divine girl who had no husband,
> How did she bear nine sons?
> Where do the spirits of Pestilence and Peace abide?
> How does shutting bring darkness,

> And opening bring light?
> Before the dawn-star appears,
> Where does the sun hide its beams?
> If Kun could not deal with the Flood,
> Why did the people esteem him?

Here follows a passage on the great inundation, which some, as already mentioned, have sought to identify with the Noachian Deluge. An officer, named Kun, was first instructed by the Emperor Yao to take it in hand; but after nine years he had accomplished nothing, and the work was entrusted by the next Emperor, Shun, to the Great Yü, who, as we have before seen, carried it to a successful issue. Although it is quite out of the question that this Chinese Flood and the Deluge of the Old Testament can have had any connexion one with the other, still, it is a curious coincidence that China should have suffered from an inundation of such severity that it made quite as deep an impression upon the minds of the Chinese people as was made by the Deluge upon the minds of the Jewish people, and perhaps with equal exaggerations in both cases. Even at the present day, the two catastrophes, embalmed as they are in the sacred books of each nation, are equally familiar to both peoples. "All the high hills," says the Jewish account, "that were under the whole heaven, were covered." "The waters of the Flood," say the Chinese, "rose to the sky."

The poem rambles on to a considerable length, with questions on the myths and popular beliefs of ancient China, such as,

> Where is the forest of stone trees,
> And the animals that can speak?
> Where is the country in which men do not die,
> And that in which the long-armed people live?
> How big is the serpent which can swallow elephants?
> When do the lives end of those who do not die?

In several places God is mentioned; once as sending down a substitute for a wicked ruler, and again as refusing to accept the fat of sacrifice, in view of the irregular prayer with which it was accompanied. We are also told that

> The will of God is inconsistent,

sometimes punishing the good, sometimes protecting the wicked, of which statement the poet quotes several historical examples. For the word "God," *Shang Ti* is used once; otherwise, *T'ien* is employed, or Ti as an abbreviation of *Shang Ti*.

This singular poem was dealt with by Liu Tsung-yüan, a distinguished poet, who flourished in the eighth and ninth centuries of our era and published a set of "God Answers" to the famous questions, "of which," as a native critic has said, "he missed the real purport." For myself, I freely confess to missing the purport of a great many of the replies, which are wrapped up in exceedingly obscure language; while such as are easily intelligible, seem to be trivial. For instance, in reply to the question how it was that a divine girl who had no husband bore nine sons, the answer simply amounts to "because she was divine"; and the question how shutting brings darkness and opening brings light, meets with a direct denial that such is the case. We may therefore dismiss further reference to "God Answers," the author of which we shall meet again later on.

Ch'ü P'ing believed in divination, and he has left on record an account of his experiences when trying to probe the future. Three years had elapsed since his dismissal from office, and still he was unable to obtain an audience of his prince. His fervent loyalty had been intercepted by the tongue of slander. He was broken in spirit, and knew not whither to direct his steps. In his doubt he repaired to the Chief Augur and asked for a response. Thereupon the Chief Augur arranged the divining-reeds and wiped the tortoise-shell, saying, "What, sir, are the points on which you desire to be enlightened?"

"Tell me," cried Ch'ü P'ing, "whether I should steadily pursue the path of truth and loyalty, or follow in the wake of a corrupt generation. Should I work in the fields with spade and hoe, or seek advancement in the retinue of a grandee? Should I rest content in the cultivation of virtue, or practise the art of wheedling women in order to secure success? Should I be pure and clean-handed in my rectitude, or be an oily-mouthed, slippery, timeserving sycophant? Should I hold on my course like an impetuous charger, or oscillate to and fro, with the indecision of a duck in a pool, as self-interest directs? Should I vie with the wild goose in soaring to heaven, or scramble for food on a dunghill with hens? Of these alternatives I would know which to choose. The age is muddy and will not be made clean. The wing of the cicada outweighs a thousand pounds. The priceless goblet is set aside for the delf cup. Flatterers fill high places; men of worth are ignored. Alas! who is there that knows my worth?"

The Chief Augur gathered up his divining apparatus and saluted Ch'ü P'ing, saying, "A foot is ofttimes too short; an inch, too long. The implements of my art are inadequate to your requirements. Think for yourself, and translate your thoughts into action. The divining-reeds and the tortoise-shell would avail you naught."

T'an Kung, the writer of the fourth and third centuries B.C. from whom we have already taken a note on the custom of burying people alive, provides further sidelights upon such topics as ordinary burial and mourning. "A certain man," he says, "travelled from afar to witness the funeral obsequies of Confucius. He stayed at the house of a disciple, who observed that a sage conducting a funeral is one thing, and that a sage's funeral is another, and asked the visitor what he had expected to see. 'Do you not remember,' said the disciple, 'that our Master once said, "Some persons pile up the earth over graves into square, others into long-shaped tumuli. Others are content with small heaps. I prefer the small heaps"? So we have given him only a few handfuls of earth, and he is already buried. Is not this as he would have wished it himself?'"

The question of mourning is treated by T'an Kung as follows: "One day, Yu-tzŭ and Tzŭ-yu, two of Confucius' disciples, happened to see a child weeping for the loss of its parents. Thereupon the former said, 'I never could understand why mourners should necessarily jump about to show their grief; I would long ago have got rid of the custom. Now here you have an honest expression of feeling, and that is all there should ever be.'

"'My friend,' replied Tzŭ-yu, 'the mourning ceremonial, with all its material accompaniments, is at once a check upon undue emotion and a guarantee against any lack of proper respect. Simply to give vent to the feelings is the way of barbarians. That is not our way.

"'Consider. A man who is pleased will show it in his face. He will sing. He will get excited. He will dance. So, too, a man who is vexed will look sad. He will sigh. He will beat his breast. He will jump about. The due regulation of these emotions is the function of a set ceremonial.

"'Further, a man dies and becomes an object of loathing. A dead body is shunned. Therefore a shroud is prepared, and other paraphernalia of burial, in order that the survivors may cease to loathe. At death there is a sacrifice of wine and meat; when the funeral procession is about to start there is another; and after burial there is yet a third sacrifice. Yet no one has ever seen the spirit of the departed come to taste the food.

"'These have been our customs from remote antiquity. They have not been discarded, because, in consequence, men no more shun the dead. What you may censure in those who perform the ceremonial is no blemish in the ceremonial itself.'"

The same writer introduces into the same subject the question of a divorced mother. He tells how the son of Tzŭ-ssŭ, the grandson of Confucius, who had divorced his wife, refused to attend the funeral of his divorced mother, and how his father was interrogated by one of his own disciples, saying, "Did not *your* father attend *his* divorced mother's funeral (alluding to the divorced wife of Confucius), and if so, why cannot you make your son do likewise?" "My grandfather," replied Tzŭ-ssŭ, "was a man of complete virtue. With him, whatever was, was right. I cannot aspire to his level. For me, so long as the deceased was my wife, she was my son's mother. When she ceased to be my wife, she ceased also to be his mother." From that time forth, it became the rule among the descendants of Confucius not to attend the funeral of a divorced mother.

Three divorces in four generations of the same family might lead to the inference that divorce has always been common in China; but whatever may have been the case in ancient times, of which even the most meagre statistics are wanting, it is quite certain that nowadays divorce, which has always been justified under certain conditions, is of very rare occurrence. The lady's family has to be reckoned with, and her relatives and friends take care that justice is done. Premising that, in China, the dog has always been regarded as an unclean animal, and is used as a term of abuse, we read that a man, named Pao Yung, who lived about the time of the Christian era, has ever since been lauded for his filial piety, because he divorced his wife, somewhat harshly as we should think, for calling her mother-in-law a bitch.

On the subject of mourning and funeral rites, there is a story told by T'an Kung of Confucius, generally stigmatized as a formalist and an inveterate stickler for etiquette, which shows the Master in a somewhat broader light. An old friend having lost his mother, Confucius went to assist in varnishing the coffin. "Well, well," exclaimed the friend, "'tis long since I have had any music." Thereupon he began to sing—a grave breach of Chinese decorum. Confucius pretended not to hear, and moved away; but one of his disciples cried out, "Master! should you not have done with a fellow like this?" "It is certainly not right," replied Confucius, "to disregard the duties we owe to our parents; but neither is it right to disregard the duties we owe to our friends."

The last quarter of the third century B.C. witnessed the final disappearance of the Feudal System, which had endured, with more or less vigour, for the long period of over eight hundred years. China now became an empire, under the self-named "First Emperor," whose successors were to be called Second, Third, Fourth, and so on, for ever. We need not here linger over the historical fact that the Second Emperor was deposed and put to death, thus bringing the Chin dynasty, as it was styled, to an early end; but it is necessary, in order to a full understanding of the literature and religion of China, to mention an extraordinary event which occurred under the preceding reign. The First Emperor, about B.C. 212, issued instructions, at the suggestion of his prime minister, that all records of previous dynasties and all copies of existing books, with the exception of those on medicine, divination, or agriculture, should be forthwith burned. The advice was given partly out of flattery to the Emperor, from whose reign literature and history would take a fresh start, and partly with a view of strengthening the recently established house. It was immediately put into force as law, and subsequently several hundred scholars were buried alive for their disobedience in concealing forbidden volumes. Thus perished many valuable works; and it was only by stealth that others, including the prohibited portions of the Confucian Canon—the Canon of Changes being classified as a work on divination—were hidden away by devoted enthusiasts, and subsequently discovered and preserved for future ages. In fact, so soon after the catastrophe did the revival take place, that scholars were still to be found who could repeat large portions of certain books by heart. This was all as it should be; unfortunately, however, the opportunity was seized by evil-disposed persons to "recover" various works, some of which had actually been destroyed in the great holocaust, or had already disappeared by mere efflux of time, and others which had never previously existed at all. An era of forgery set in, and of skilful forgery too, but not sufficiently skilful to defy the acumen of critics of a later age. This is all that it is necessary to say at the moment in reference to the Burning of the Books.

In our present connexion, this Emperor plays an important part as having been the first monarch to ascend and worship Mt. T'ai in Shantung, which is one, and in a religious sense the most important, of the five sacred mountains of China.[1] By this date, the old monotheism, with its associated worship of spiritual ancestors, had become extensively overlaid with various forms of nature worship. The sun, moon, and stars had long shared with rivers, mountains, trees, thunder, the house-door, the hearth, etc., etc., in the propitiatory sacrifices and prayers which had once been offered to God and to ancestors alone. Great heights have always had an attraction of their own, with perhaps a special appeal in reference to supernatural phenomena. An old poet of the T'ang dynasty (Liu Yü-hsi, A.D. 772-842) says,

> Hills are not famous for height alone;
> 'Tis the Genius Loci that gives them their charm.

Mt. T'ai forms no exception to the rule. It is, in fact, a divinity, manifesting itself from time to time under human form. Five centuries before Christ, the story goes that a prince of the Ch'i State, that is, of modern Shantung, saw in a dream two men who appeared to be violently enraged, and he was told by an augur that they were the spirits of Mt. T'ai, angry because the prince's army had passed the mountain without offering the usual sacrifice. No explanation is given of the two spirits, who ever afterwards were content to be worshipped as a single being. The chief favours sought from the mountain were (1) rain and fine weather in due season, in order to produce abundant crops for the farmer, and food for the people at large; (2) protection from earthquakes, thunder-storms, and such dangers as were supposed to be connected with the appearance of comets, eclipses, and other natural phenomena. In addition to these occasions of entering into communication with the spirit of the mountain, some Emperors thought it advisable to announce their accession to the throne, as a policy of conciliation in advance.

Approval and assistance were also invoked in the event of a campaign in distant regions, with a view to the preservation of life as well from the risks

---

[1] See *Le T'ai Chan*, by Prof. E. Chavannes.

of disease as from death and wounds in the ordinary course of war. Prayers, many of which are still extant, were addressed to the mountain, not as an independent deity whose fiat was all that it was necessary to obtain, but as a mediator between God and man, and one especially well situated by virtue of elevation to convey human entreaties to the far-off Supreme Ruler in the sky. On the other hand, the mountain was saddled with full responsibility for the success of the negotiations between God and man. One Emperor, so late as 1455, to anticipate chronological order, made this quite clear in his address, as follows: "If it is through my wrong-doings that I have drawn down these calamities, I shall not indeed seek to escape from personal responsibility; but in the matter of changing misfortune into happiness, it is really you, O divine one, whose duty it is to attend to that. If after my error you fail to bring about a satisfactory issue, you will then he as guilty as I am; but if, on the contrary, you change misfortune into happiness, whose merit will be equal to yours?" Again, on the occasion of a disastrous flood, the same Emperor addresses the mountain in similar terms: "Upon whom rests the responsibility? Undoubtedly, this calamity is due to my lack of virtue; but you too, O divine one, how can you escape from blame? It is your business to see that, when the waters burst forth, profit may ensue, and that they may be for the advantage and not for the distress of the people. Thus, both you and I will have done our duty; in the eyes of God we shall have committed no crime, and in the eyes of the people there will be nothing for which we need blush."

The east is regarded by the Chinese as the source of life; it is from that quarter that the sun daily renews its light, after being nightly extinguished in the waves of the western sea. Mt. T'ai dominates the east; and consequently, when an Emperor desired a son, it was to this mountain that he addressed his prayer: "From of old, your divine influence has been concentrated upon the production of life. You dominate one quarter of the empire, and secretly give assistance to the State. I, with all my imperfections, have now for eleven years been the respectful depositary of the will of God, and during this period I have reverently served the spirits of heaven and earth without any neglect. I have no heir, and this causes me constant anxiety. Therefore I have specially prepared a fitting offering, to wit, a sacrificial animal, silk, unfermented wine, and vegetables, and I have deputed an officer to convey this humble prayer, hoping that by virtue of your supernatural power you will obtain for me an heir, and thus prolong the happiness and duration of my line, and at the same time secure to yourself the blessing of sacrificial worship for ever and ever."

Some of the still extant prayers addressed to the mountain read more like invocations of God Himself. For instance, one prayer opens thus: "O Thou Spirit, who since the beginning of the world hast ruled with might over the eastern quarter, who bringest the clouds and the rain, and dost nourish in abundance all living creatures, etc., etc."

The functions of Mt. T'ai have not been restricted to care for the living; at a very early date the mountain came to be regarded as the rendezvous of the dead, whose souls found their way thither after death, and settled down on a small hill hard by, where relatives often put up tablets to their memory. This connexion with the dead gave rise to the belief that the mountain was in some way an arbiter of human existence, in consequence of which it became customary to address to the spirit prayers for the prolongation of life.

The ascent of Mt. T'ai by the First Emperor seems to have been nothing more than an incident, as compared with a similar ascent, B.C. 110, by Wu Ti of the Han dynasty, one of China's most famous Emperors, whose long reign extended from B.C. 140 down to B.C. 86. Wu Ti decided that the ceremony should not be a public one, and he took with him to the summit of the mountain a single official only. Why this secrecy should have been practised is not actually known. It has been suggested that the Emperor's object was to obtain for himself happiness and longevity, and to divert to his attendant, as a scapegoat, any possible misfortunes in the future which might otherwise fall to his own lot. The point in question will always remain a mystery; within a few days the attendant was suddenly taken ill and died, leaving no one behind, except the Emperor, who could say what had actually taken place.

Upon four more occasions, at intervals of several years, this same Emperor repeated his pilgrimage to the top of Mt. T'ai; and his example was followed by the Emperor Kuang Wu of the Later Han dynasty in A.D. 56; by the Emperors Kao Tsung and Hsüan Tsung, both of the T'ang dynasty, in A.D. 666 and 725 respectively; by the Emperor Chên Tsung of the Sung dynasty in A.D. 1008, an account of which will be given in its more chronological place; and finally by the vigorous Manchu Emperor K'ang Hsi in 1684. Gradually there grew up two definite services of religious rites and ceremonies, known as *fêng* and *shan*, the former consisting of sacrifices to God as father, and the latter of sacrifices to Earth as mother, of all living things. On arrival at the foot of Mt. T'ai, the worshipper began by a preliminary sacrifice at a special altar on a small hill, in order to announce to the spirit that the ascent of the mountain was about to be made. The more important sacrifice was reserved for the summit, on which a second altar—both were round in shape—had been prepared on a larger scale. A similar sacrifice to Mother Earth was also performed on the summit, and a second sacrifice, after descending, on an octagonal altar built on another small hill at the foot of Mt. T'ai. For the *fêng* ceremonial the offerings were burnt, as in ordinary sacrificial worship, so that they might be carried up by fire and smoke into the presence of God; for the *shan* ceremonial in honour of Mother Earth, the offerings were buried. These rites were no longer personal on the part of the Emperor concerned, that is, performed with an eye to individual benefits, such as happiness and long life; their chief object was to acknowledge to God and to Mother Earth, through the medium of the mountain spirit, the blessings which had been vouchsafed to the reigning house, and to render thanks for the same. This fact was recorded by inscriptions on two tablets of jade, which were carefully enclosed in two stone chests and then deposited, one on the summit of Mt. T'ai, to be communicated to God, and the other on the *shan* hill at the foot of the mountain, to be communicated to Mother Earth.

The worship of Mt. T'ai, to which we shall return in a future lecture, has spread all over China, and temples dedicated to its spirit are to be found in most large towns. Any worshipper may now approach these shrines, and offer up his commonplace prayers. It was not always so. When, in the days of Confucius, the head of a powerful clan proposed to sacrifice to Mt. T'ai, the Master was horrified that a vassal should venture to usurp the rights of his suzerain. He consoled himself, however, by reflecting that the spirit of the mountain would assuredly resent the affront.

It will be convenient here to say a few words about another minor deity, whose worship dates from early ages, and is still, with such modifications as time brings about, in the forefront of Chinese religious life. We need not accept too literally the native tradition that agriculture was first taught to the Chinese by an inspired Emperor who lived some thirty centuries before the Christian era; on the other hand, we may take it for certain that so soon as it became a matter of routine to extract from the earth a much more satisfactory livelihood than could be obtained from berries and fruits, a desire to secure regular supplies would naturally suggest to man's growing intelligence the deification of the source of supply and some form of propitiatory recognition. It was thus that the agriculturalist came to look upon the earth—not the whole earth as contrasted with the sky, but his own particular portion of the soil—as a conscious being, able to provide at will for his daily necessities, and amenable to the soft flattery of sacrifice and prayer. The soil, with its apparent powers of yielding or withholding its vegetable products, became a god—a fifth among the cluster of family deities, the gods of the kitchen-stove, of the well, of the front door, and of the parlour. The god of the soil once had his seat in every house, below a small hole in the roof which admitted both light and especially rain, for the latter of which it was necessary to preserve an uninterrupted line of communication with the sky. We are told that this hole originated with underground dwellings built in layers, one over another; but in such case it is more than probable that the god of the soil had nothing to do with the matter, even if he had ever been heard of by the inhabitants of such primitive homes. However this may be, it was of paramount importance that the altar of the god should be without roof or covering of any kind; and thus these altars were always built, as by degrees the worship ceased to be an individual rite and became a public rite, until first villages and later large cities possessed altars which belonged to the people in common. When, in 1766 B.C., T'ang the Completer had destroyed the last evil Emperor of the dynasty of Hsia, he wished to remove the altar of the god of the soil who had been associated with the rulers of that time; but he found that this plan would be undesirable, for technical reasons. Being a man of resources, he speedily hit upon means to achieve the end in view. He put a roof over the spot, and from that moment all spirituality was gone. The roofed altar was preserved, as a reminder of the justice of God.

Worship of the god of the soil may still be seen nightly in any Chinese city. At the doors of shops and houses, lighted sticks of incense are set before small stone tablets which record the presence of the god, worshipped here no longer for agricultural assistance, but for anything that can be got out of him.

The attempt to deal chronologically with traces of the genuinely religious feelings of the Chinese people has brought us, with some necessary anticipations, down to the time of the Christian era, or thereabouts. We must now break off what is meant to be the main thread of these lectures in order to deal with other strands of thought, which have for many centuries largely influenced, and do still largely influence, the religious life of the Chinese.

B.C. 200-A.D. 100

SCATTERED through the genuine remains of certain Chinese philoso-phers who flourished in the fourth, third, and second centuries B.C., we find a number of pithy sayings and maxims attributed to a personage named Lao Tzŭ. Various accounts have been given of the date, place, and manner of his birth, all of which bear the stamp of legend. Some say that his mother was moved by a shooting star, under which form he came down from heaven. Some say that he came into being before the universe, and some that he was the quintessential spirit of God. Others speak of a gestation of seventy-two years, at the end of which he emerged from his mother's side; others again declare that his was a case of virgin birth. The name Lao Tzŭ is usually accepted as meaning Old Philosopher; it may also mean "old child," which latter term has been adopted by some and explained by the fact that this child's hair was white at birth, or alternatively, by a *lucus a non lucendo* process, that he was called Old Boy because, although existing before the universe, he never became old. All this does not by any means prove that no such man as Lao Tzŭ ever existed. The conviction which must be forced upon the minds of all who have given serious attention to the subject lies in an exactly contrary direction; the real difficulty is with the date of Lao Tzŭ's birth, now popularly, but not authoritatively, fixed at 604 B.C.

An effort has been made, by the usual trick of interpolation, to show that Confucius paid a visit to Lao Tzŭ, and was astounded at the wisdom of the Old Philosopher. In addition to the chronological difficulty, those who favour this view have to explain away the awkward fact that Confucius never once mentions the name of Lao Tzŭ; neither does the writer of the commentary to the Confucian annals, whose record covers Lao Tzŭ's lifetime; neither does Mencius, who made it the chief business of his life to exalt Confucianism and to demolish the system of any possible competitor. The first writer of real consequence who does mention Lao Tzŭ's name, and the genuineness of whose work as a whole—for chapters and paragraphs have been interpolated—is above suspicion, lived in the fourth and third centuries B.C., and is known as Chuang Tzŭ, the philosopher Chuang, already quoted in connexion with the impersonator of the dead. He attempted to substitute Lao Tzŭ, as the spiritual guide of the Chinese people, for Confucius, whose teachings he considered likely to bring about the very evils they were intended to combat. Except in passages where Lao Tzŭ is actually mentioned, it is often impossible to say how far Chuang Tzŭ has drawn his inspiration from the older philosopher, and how far his speculations are his own. He had only tradition to help him; it was not until a much later date that a book, said to be by Lao Tzŭ, appeared in literature. This book will be dealt with in its place; meanwhile, we may consider a few passages from the writings of Chuang Tzŭ himself, who strove to do for the doctrines of Lao Tzŭ what Mencius did for Confucianism.

"Joy and anger," says Chuang Tzŭ, "sorrow and happiness, caution and remorse, come upon us by turns, with ever-changing mood. They come like music from hollowness, like mushrooms from damp. Daily and nightly they alternate within us, but we cannot tell whence they spring. Can we then hope in a moment to lay a finger upon their very Cause? But for these emotions, *I* should not be. But for me, *they* would have no scope. So far can we go; but we do not know what it is that brings them into play. 'Twould seem to be a soul; but the clue to its existence is wanting. That some Power operates is credible enough, though we cannot see its form. Perhaps it has functions without form. Take the human body with all its manifold divisions. Which part of it does a man love best? Does he not cherish all equally, or has he a preference? Do not all equally serve him? And do these servitors then govern themselves, or are they subdivided into rulers and subjects? Surely there is some soul that sways them all. But whether or not we ascertain what are the functions of this soul, it matters but little to the soul itself. For coming into existence with this mortal coil of mine, with the exhaustion of this mortal coil the mandate of the soul will be exhausted. To be harassed by the wear and tear of life, and to pass rapidly through it without the possibility of arresting one's course—is not this pitiful indeed? To labour without ceasing, and then, without living to enjoy the fruit, worn out, to depart suddenly, one knows not whither—is not that a just cause for grief?"

Chuang Tzŭ conceived of the soul as an emanation from God, passing to and from this earth through the portals of birth and death. Life was not a boon, but rather a misfortune, banishing the recipient, for a longer or shorter period, from partnership with God. Death was therefore a release, enabling the wearied spirit to return whence it had come. But the God of Chuang Tzŭ was no longer identical with the God of the Odes, though here and there traces of the old conception remain.

We are sometimes confronted with a psychological Unity instead of a concrete personality. With Chuang Tzŭ, all things are one, and that One is God, in whose obliterating unity we are embraced. "What is it," he asks, "to be embraced in the obliterating unity of God? It is this. With reference to positive and negative, to that which is so and that which is not so—if the positive is really positive, it must necessarily be different from its negative: there is no room for argument. And if that which is so really is so, it must necessarily be different from that which is not so: there is no room for argument." Therefore we are advised to take no heed of time, nor of right and wrong, but, passing into the realm of the Infinite, that is, of God, to take our final rest therein. Contraries, he explains, cannot but exist, but they should exist independently of each other, without antagonism. Such a condition is found only in the all-embracing unity of God; in other words, of the Infinite Absolute. There, all distinctions of positive and negative, of right and wrong, of this and that, are obliterated and merged in One. But this still leaves us far from the desired goal. According to Herbert Spencer (*Principles of Psychology*, i. p. 272), "The antithesis of subject and object, never to be transcended while consciousness lasts, renders impossible all knowledge of the Ultimate Reality in which subject and object are united." Chuang Tzŭ, however, has an illustration which, if it fails to prove that the antithesis of subject and object may indeed be transcended, has had at any rate the merit of gaining for its author the sobriquet of "Butterfly Chuang." It is brief, and to the point. "Once upon a time, I dreamt I was a butterfly, fluttering hither and thither, to all intents and purposes a butterfly. Suddenly I awaked, and there I lay, myself again. Now I do not know whether I was then a man dreaming I was a butterfly, or whether I am now a butterfly dreaming I am a man."

"He who knows what God is," says Chuang Tzŭ, "and who knows what man is, has attained. Knowing what God is, he knows that he himself proceeded therefrom. Knowing what man is, he rests in the knowledge of the known, waiting for the knowledge of the unknown. Herein, however, there is a flaw. Knowledge is dependent upon fulfilment. And as this fulfilment is uncertain, how can it be known that my divine is not really human, my human really divine?" By these words Chuang Tzŭ means that not until death lifts the veil can we truly know that this life is bounded at each end by an immortality from which the soul originally came and to which it finally reverts, thereby admitting that his dogma is no more than a human speculation, and certainly not of the nature of a revelation from God Himself. He goes on to say that it is all-important for us to have men of transcendent knowledge, such indeed as were the men of old. "For what they cared for could be reduced to One, and what they did not care for to One also. That which was One was One, and that which was not One was likewise One. In that which was One, they were of God; in that which was not One, they were of man. And so between the human and the divine no conflict ensued." Confucius, who is frequently introduced by Chuang Tzŭ into imaginary conversations, is here made to confirm this view. The occasion was an historical one, and is mentioned in the Analects (Lun Yü). Confucius and his disciples were in danger, while travelling, and had been some days—Chuang Tzŭ says seven days—without food. In the Analects we have merely a complaint by one of the disciples, rebuked by Confucius, that superior men should have to suffer privations. Chuang Tzŭ represents Confucius as singing, to relieve the tension, and stopping to say to one of the disciples, There is no beginning and no end. Man and God are One. That being the case, who was singing just now?" In another passage we read, "The ultimate end is God. He is manifested in the laws of nature. He is the hidden spring. At the beginning, He was. This, however," Chuang Tzŭ adds, "is inexplicable. It is unknowable. But from the unknowable we reach the known."

After this, it may be a surprise to find that God was not the ultimate Supreme Power recognized by Chuang Tzŭ, as an exponent of the doctrines of Lao Tzŭ. In spite of the lofty position accorded, as we have seen, to God, there was something—we cannot say someone—on which Chuang Tzŭ, following Lao Tzŭ, made God Himself dependent, not only for power, but even for His very existence. This something was called by Lao Tzŭ *Tao*, meaning, as it means in common parlance to this day, a way, a road, a path. In Confucianism it is used for the true path, like the ὁδός of the New Testament, or the Buddhist *marga*, the path which leads to Nirvâna; and it subsequently comes to mean doctrines, and even religion. Han Fei, a philosopher of the third century B.C., tells us that matter which is subject to structural changes cannot be regarded as eternal; it came into being with heaven and earth, and with heaven and earth it will pass away. But the eternal is unconditioned; and therefore it was that Lao Tzŭ explained, in reference to *Tao*, "The way which can be walked upon is not the eternal Way."

To translate the *Tao* of Lao Tzŭ and of Chuang Tzŭ by the Way, is, as will be shown, a mere makeshift; the word is untranslatable. Chuang Tzŭ says, "A man looks upon God as his father, and loves Him in like measure. Shall he, then, not love that which is greater than God?"—meaning Tao, the omnipresent, omnipotent, eternal something which invests even God Himself with the power and attributes of divinity. In the words of Chuang Tzǔ, "Tao has its laws, and its evidences. It is devoid both of action and of form. It may be transmitted, but cannot be taken. It may be obtained, but cannot be seen. Before heaven and earth were, Tao was. It has existed without change from all time. Spiritual beings drew their spirituality therefrom, while the universe became what we see it now. To Tao, the zenith is not high, nor the nadir low; no point in time is long ago, nor by lapse of ages has Tao itself grown old."

Chuang Tzǔ proceeds to enumerate several famous sovereigns and others of antiquity who, by virtue of *Tao*, succeeded in all their undertakings. Among these he includes some striking and familiar objects in nature. "The constellation of the Great Bear obtained *Tao*, and has never erred from its course. The sun and moon obtained it, and have never ceased to revolve." We have now to face the apparent paradox that although *Tao* can be obtained, nevertheless it cannot be taught. Of this Chuang Tzǔ gives several illustrative anecdotes. A man who was asked how in old age he still managed to keep the complexion of a child, replied that it was the result of *Tao*; and he went on to say that in a case in which he had caused a pupil to become, so to speak, possessed by *Tao*, he had succeeded, not by teaching but by not teaching. "I imparted," he explained, "as though withholding; and within three days, for him, this sublunary state (with all its paltry distinctions of sovereign and subject, high and low, good and bad, etc.) had ceased to exist. When he had attained to this, I withheld again; and in seven days more, for him, the external world had ceased to be. And so again for another nine days, when he became unconscious of his own self. He was first etherealized, next possessed of perfect wisdom, then without past or present, and finally able to enter there where life and death are no more, where killing does not take away life, nor does the prolongation of life add to the duration of existence."

Chuang Tzǔ is the greatest of the heterodox writers of China. His work is highly esteemed for its trenchant and beautiful style, but it is none the less under the ban of the orthodox. The reason for this is obvious. Confucianism is satirized, and Confucius himself is held up to ridicule as unable to refute the doctrine of *Tao*, and even becoming a convert to its tenets. Chuang Tzǔ invents a story of three men who were conversing together, when it was asked, "Who can be, and yet not be? Who can do, and yet not do? Who can mount to heaven, and, roaming through the clouds, pass beyond the limits of space, oblivious of existence, for ever and ever without end?" The three looked at each other and smiled; and as neither had any misgivings, they became friends accordingly. Shortly afterwards, one of them, named Sang Hu, died; whereupon Confucius sent a disciple to take part in the mourning. The disciple found one of the two survivors playing on a psaltery, or Chinese lute, and the other singing,

> La, la, la—come back to us, Sang Hu (*calling his spirit*).
> Thou hast already returned to thy God,
> While we still remain here as men—alas!

"How can you sing," cried the disciple, "alongside of a corpse? Is this decorum?" The two looked at each other and laughed, saying, What should this man know of decorum indeed?" The disciple then hurried back and reported to Confucius, who said, "These men travel beyond the rule of life. I travel within it. Consequently our paths do not meet; and I was wrong in sending you to mourn. They consider themselves as one with God, recognizing no distinctions between human and divine. They look on life as a huge tumour from which death sets them free. All the same, they know not where they were before birth, nor where they will be after death. Though admitting different elements, they take their stand upon the unity of all things. They ignore their passions. They take no count of their ears and eyes. Backward and forward through all eternity, they do not admit a beginning or an end. They stroll beyond the dust and dirt of mortality, to wander in the realms of inaction. How should such men trouble themselves with the conventionalities of this world, or care what people may think of them?" "But if this is the case," said the disciple, "why should we stick to the old rule?" "God has condemned me to this," replied Confucius; "nevertheless you and I may perhaps escape from it."

This last sentiment, from the mouth of the Master, would be sufficiently shocking to any devout Confucianist, but is as nothing compared with another episode, to appreciate which a few preliminary remarks may be necessary, to recall certain facts which bear upon the situation. Confucius founded his teachings upon charity of heart, duty towards one's neighbour, wisdom, and truth, with such adventitious aids to morality as music and ceremonies. But Chuang Tzŭ, expounding the doctrines of Lao Tzŭ, taught that all restrictions are artificial, and therefore deceptive; only by shaking off such fetters, and reverting to the natural, could man hope to attain. He maintained that distinctions of right and wrong, of *meum* and *tuum*, and other ethical refinements, were but the inventions of philosophers, and would have no place under simple conditions of existence. To quote a single instance, he argued that if all scales and measures were destroyed, the people would cease at once to wrangle over quantities, and the result would be the victory of *Tao*. We may now approach the episode.

"I am getting on," observed a favourite disciple to Confucius. "How so?" asked the latter. "I have got rid of charity of heart and duty towards my neighbour," replied the disciple. "Very good," said Confucius, "but not perfect." Another day the disciple met Confucius again and said, "I am getting on." "How so?" asked Confucius. "I have got rid of music and ceremonies." "Very good," said Confucius, "but not perfect." On a third occasion the two met once more, and the disciple said, "I am getting on." "How so?" asked Confucius, as before. "I have got rid of everything," replied the disciple. "Got rid of everything!" cried Confucius eagerly, "what do you mean by that?" "I have freed myself from my body," said the disciple. "I have discarded my reasoning powers. And by thus getting rid of both body and mind, I have become One with the Infinite." "In that case," said Confucius, "I trust to be allowed to follow in your steps."

There is a rather fascinating chapter in which Chuang Tzǔ employs allegory to aid in the elucidation of *Tao*. Knowledge set forth on his travels, and meeting Do-nothing Say-nothing, thus addressed him: "Kindly tell me by what thoughts, by what cogitations, may *Tao* be known? By resting in what, by according with what, by pursuing what, may *Tao* be attained?" Getting no answer, he went off, and by and by meeting All-in-extremes, he put the same questions. "Ha!" cried All-in-extremes, "I know; I will tell you. . . ." But just as he was about to speak, he forgot what he wanted to say. So Knowledge proceeded to the Imperial palace and asked the Yellow Emperor (B.C. 2698), who is often associated with Lao Tzǔ as an exponent of *Tao*, and even as a contemporary, though separated, according to received chronology, by some two thousand years. "By having no thoughts, by having no cogitations," answered the Yellow Emperor, "*Tao* can be known. By resting in nothing, by according with nothing, Tao can be approached. By following nothing, by pursuing nothing, *Tao* can be obtained." And he added, "Those who understand, do not speak; those who speak, do not understand. Therefore the inspired man teaches a doctrine which does not find expression in words." These last two sentences have been attributed to Lao Tzǔ, and constitute the basis of his doctrine of Silence; but the authority of Chuang Tzǔ is too great to be lightly brushed aside.

The still more famous doctrine of Inaction—Do nothing and all things will be done—which is also attributed to Lao Tzǔ, appears in Chuang Tzǔ as an actual utterance by the Yellow Emperor. The doctrine itself is discussed in several passages. For instance: "I make true happiness consist in inaction. Thus, perfect happiness is the absence of happiness." This seems to mean that the non-existence of any state or condition necessarily includes the non-existence of its correlate. If we do not have happiness, we are at once exempt from misery; and such a negative state is a state of perfect happiness. Again, "To act through inaction is God," so excellent are the results achieved, especially, we are told, in government. In an allegorical passage Chuang Tzǔ makes the Vital Principle say, "That the scheme of empire is in confusion, that the proper conditions of life are violated, that the will of God does not triumph, that the beasts of the field are disorganized, that the birds of the air cry at night, that blight reaches the trees and herbs, that destruction spreads among creeping things—this, alas! is the fault of governing. Rest in inaction, and the world will be good of itself. Cast your slough. Spit forth intelligence. Ignore all differences. Become one with the Infinite. Release your mind. Free your soul. Be vacuous. Be nothing!"

We find a sudden transition to more practical politics in an answer which Lao Tzǔ is supposed to have given to one who asked him, saying, "If the empire is not to be governed, how are men's hearts to be kept in order?" "Be careful," replied Lao Tzǔ, "not to interfere with the natural goodness of the heart of man. Man's heart may be forced down or stirred up; in each case the issue is fatal. By gentleness the hardest heart may be softened. But try to cut and polish it;—'twill glow like fire or freeze like ice. In the twinkling of an eye it will pass beyond the Four Seas. In repose, profoundly still; in motion, far away in the sky. No bolt can bar, no bond can bind;—such is the human heart."

Among other philosophers who quote sayings by Lao Tzǔ may be mentioned a grandson of the founder of the Han dynasty, known as the. prince of Huai-nan. He died in 122 B.C., leaving behind him a large work, the first chapter of which is devoted to the origin of *Tao*, and the rest to what we may now begin to call the doctrines of Taoism. "*Tao*," he says, "covers the sky, and supports the earth; it stretches to, and includes, the four quarters and the eight boundaries of space; its height cannot be measured, nor its depth fathomed;" and so on. Among the sayings of Lao Tzŭ he quotes these words; "Follow diligently *Tao* in your own heart, but make no display of it to the world," which may be compared with an almost identical utterance by Christ: "Take heed that ye do not your righteousness before men, to be seen of them." Another saying is, "He who, knowing himself to be strong, is content to be weak—he shall be a cynosure of men." Again, "The softest things in the world override the hardest; that which has no substance enters where there is no crevice. And so I know that there is advantage in Inaction." In illustration of this last, the prince of Huai-nan borrowed, without acknowledgment, the following anecdote from Chuang Tzŭ: "Light asked Nothing if it really existed or not. Nothing did not answer, so Light set to work to watch it. All of a sudden, he could not see it, or hear it, or touch it. 'Bravo!' cried Light. 'Who is equal to that? I can get to be nothing, but I cannot get to be not nothing.'" Chuang Tzŭ himself gives another short anecdote in which "nothing" is made to take the part of Inaction. The Yellow Emperor, he tells us, having lost his magic pearl, employed Intelligence to find it, but without success. He then employed Sight, and next Speech, but in each case without success. Finally he employed Nothing, and Nothing got it. The key to this is that he did not employ Nothing *to find the pearl*. He simply employed Nothing.

A miracle recorded by the prince of Huai-nan shows that good Taoists get their rewards in this world as well as in the next, and also recalls the famous miracle of the sun standing still upon Gibeon, and the moon upon Ajalon. A duke of Lu-yang, described as a man of true and perfect nature, whose being was in relationship with God, happened to be at war with another State. Sunset was fast approaching, while a furious battle was still raging; and the duke, in order to gain time, shook his spear at the sun, which forthwith went back three out of the twenty-eight Chinese divisions of the zodiac. Legend has, of course, been busy with the name of the prince of Huai-nan. He is said to have discovered the elixir of life, and to have gone up to heaven in consequence. He is said, with more show of probability, to have dabbled in alchemy, the first notions of which are thought to have reached China from the province of Græco-Bactria. Alchemy is at any rate mentioned in the Historical Record under the year 133 B.C. A certain magician, who was able to do without food and possessed the art of putting off old age, addressed the reigning Emperor as follows: "Sacrifice to the stove and you will be able to summon spirits. With their aid, powdered cinnabar can be transmuted into yellow gold. When you have obtained yellow gold, you will be able to make vessels for holding food and drink; and by using these, you will secure a great prolongation of life."

From this date we have no longer to deal with the original *Tao* of Lao Tzǔ, as expounded by Chuang Tzǔ, Han Fei Tzǔ, Hsün Tzǔ, and to some extent by the prince of Huai-nan. Alchemy and the search for the elixir of life were both incorporated at an early date in the doctrines of the religion henceforth to be known as Taoism; and various forms of magic, incantations, and exorcism were soon added. A further and still greater modification has yet to be dealt with in its proper place.

The Historical Record states, under the year 140 B.C., that the Empress Dowager, grandmother of the reigning Emperor, "studied the words of the Yellow Emperor and Lao Tzǔ, and did not care for the precepts of Confucianism;" and in the history of the Han dynasty we are further told that, under the preceding reign, "the Emperor and the all Empress Dowager's family were obliged to study Tzǔ and follow his teachings." What were these "words of the Yellow Emperor and Lao Tzǔ," this "Lao Tzǔ" now to be studied by the Court in preference to Confucianism? So far, we have only heard of sayings by Lao Tzǔ, embedded in the writings of certain authors, to whom they had been handed down by tradition; we have never heard of a book. Confucius, Tso-ch'iu Ming, the writer of the commentary, and Mencius, as we have already seen, never mention Lao Tzǔ at all. Chuang Tzǔ, Han Fei Tzǔ, Hsün Tzǔ, and the prince of Huai-nan, who devote so many chapters to Lao Tzǔ and *Tao*, make no mention of a book. At the point where we` are now, that is, towards the middle of the second century B.C., we gather that not only were the words of Lao Tzǔ brought together into book form, but were canonized, in deference to the Dowager Empress, as a sacred text. From that date, we are told, began the study of the *Tao*. Official patronage however, was not just then of long duration; for in the same year under which it is recorded that the Empress Dowager "studied the words of the Yellow Emperor and Lao Tzǔ," her grandson, who had but lately mounted the throne, put a stop to the glorification of Lao Tzǔ, and reinstated Confucian doctrines.

The next stage in this inquiry into the rise and development of Taoism carries us, in point of time, hardly any further down. Ssǔ-ma Ch'ien, the father of Chinese history, must have been born about the middle of the second century B.C. The date of his death has been fixed at 87 B.C. He was the author of the Historical Record, in which, for the first time in Chinese literature, we find Lao Tzǔ mentioned as the writer of a book. The historian, after a few details as to Lao Tzǔ's birthplace and profession, in which pious interpolations are not far to seek, proceeds to relate the supposed, but impossible, interview of Confucius with Lao Tzǔ. Then comes the following passage: "In his cultivation of *Tao* and of *Tê* (which means the exemplification of *Tao*), Lao Tzǔ made self-effacement and absence of reputation his chief aims. After a long residence in Chow, he saw that the State was decaying; so he departed, and reached the frontier-pass. The warden of the pass said to him, 'Sir, as you are about to go into retirement, I earnestly beg that you will write a book for me.' Thereupon Lao Tzǔ wrote a book in two parts, on the meaning of *Tao* and *Tê*, containing five thousand words and more. After this, he departed, and no one knows what became of him."

We have such a book in "five thousand words and more," which answers, except as regards date of authorship, to the book to which Ssǔ-ma Ch'ien alludes, but which he does not appear to have seen. Different editions contain varying numbers of words, the average being about five thousand six hundred and fifty. It would be impossible to regard it as the work of Lao Tzǔ, say five and a half centuries before Christ, even if we could feel sure that Lao Tzǔ flourished at that date. For a long list of critical reasons, which cannot be reproduced here, it is practically certain that this book was pieced together, perhaps in the second century B.C., by a not too skilful forger. Sayings attributed to Lao Tzǔ were collected from all sources, and padded out with a supplementary text, which when not unintelligible is absurd. A small volume was thus produced, which, although it has not prevailed against the wit of native critics, has been quite a happy hunting-ground for the foreign student, ambitious to translate a Chinese text. Thus, it has been rendered many times into English and other European languages, with one uniform result. No two translators have ever agreed as to its meaning. Even the modern title of the book, *Tao Tê Ching*, which dates only from the sixth century A.D., has been interpreted in various senses. Po Chü-i, a famous poet of the eighth and ninth centuries, hit off the situation as follows:

> "Who know, speak not; who speak, know naught"—
> Are words from Lao Tzǔ's lore;
> If Lao Tzǔ knew, why did he speak
> Five thousand words and more?

Assuming, as seems probable, that some such personage as Lao Tzǔ, even though confused with the Yellow Emperor, did actually exist at some remote period, and that he is responsible for the more intelligible portions of the *Tao Tê Ching*, we can only conclude that he must have been one of those men whom the Chinese call "inspired," a term now reserved for the apostles of Confucianism.

The book has been divided into eighty-one chapters; and in chapter lxiii we find a command, familiar enough to Christians, but remarkable as occurring in Chinese literature at a very early date:

    Recompense injury with kindness!

with which we may compare the words of the New Testament, "Be not overcome of evil, but overcome evil with good" (Rom. xii. 21). It has already been stated that Confucius never made any allusion to Lao Tzǔ. There is, however, one passage given in his discourses with his disciples which proves that this famous doctrine, whatever may have been its source, was already matter of common knowledge. Here are the actual words: "Someone said to Confucius, 'Recompense injury with kindness. What do you think of that?' Confucius replied, 'With what then will you recompense kindness? Injury must be recompensed with justice, kindness with kindness.'" Another saying by Lao Tzǔ in the same strain runs thus: "To the good I would be good; to the not-good I would also be good, in order to make them good." At the same time it is elsewhere pointed out that "the goodness of *doing* good is not (real) goodness."

Several advanced political maxims are to be found in the *Tao Tê Ching*; for instance, "Govern a great nation as you would cook a small fish"—don't overdo it; *pas trop gouverner*, as we say. Again, "The empire is a divine trust, and may not be ruled. He who rules, ruins; he who holds by force, loses." So also there are practical injunctions for everyday life: "Put yourself behind, and the world will put you in front," "If you would take, you must first give," and others.

There are some few references to the God of the ancient Chinese. In chapter ix humility is described as the Way of God. In chapter xvi we have the following weak climax, which has not been identified as a genuine utterance, and seems, so far as one can venture to judge by the style, to come from a modern source: "He who is tolerant is just; he who is just is a king; he who is a king is God; he who is God is *Tao*; he who is *Tao* is long lasting, and will be all his life free from danger." In chapter xlvii we have, "Without going out of doors, we may know all about the empire; without looking out of window, we may behold the Way of God." Chapter lix opens with, "In governing man and in serving God, there is nothing like self-restraint."

All kinds of contentions were frowned upon by Lao Tzŭ, as we learn from many passages in Chuang Tzŭ, some of which have already been quoted. In chapter lxviii we are told that "the best soldiers do not fight," and that anyone who can free himself from the desire for such contentions is worthy to be "the peer of God," using the old phrase with which we are familiar in the Odes. In chapter lxxiii we have two, if not three, disconnected allusions, reminiscent of the Deity in ancient Chinese literature. The first is in doggerel:

> Which of us can truly state
> The cause of God Almighty's hate?

The others are (1) "The Way of God is, without contending, to win; without speaking, to get an answer; without beckoning, to cause spontaneous coming; without moving, to be skilful in planning"; and (2) "God's net is irresistible; its meshes are large, but there is no escape." In chapter lxxvii there is a curious passage which has not so far been discovered among the genuine *Fragmenta*, as quoted by known writers, yet which bears upon its face the stamp of authenticity: "The Way of God is like the drawing of a bow, which brings down the high and exalts the low"—just as in Luke i. 52 we read, "He hath put down the mighty from their seats, and exalted them of low degree." "It takes from those who have too much, and gives to those who have too little"—a statement which is in direct opposition to Christ's oft-repeated saying (Matt. xiii. 12), "Whosoever hath, to him shall be given: but whosoever hath not, from him shall be taken away even that he hath." Chapter lxxix is short and may be translated in full; it adds one more to what may be styled the Christian sentiments of the Old Philosopher: "When peace is made after great animosity, there is always a surplus of animosity left behind. Is not this wrong? Accordingly, the inspired man, when a creditor, does not exact his claim. An honest man strives to fulfil his contracts; a dishonest man, to evade them. The Way of God has no partialities; it is always on the side of the just." Chapter lxxxi has one final allusion to God: "The Way of God is profitable and not injurious." This conclusion is based upon a sentence taken from Chuang Tzŭ, which states, with reference to those who sincerely follow *Tao*, that "the more they give away, the more they have for themselves."

Such is the *Tao Tê Ching*. As a whole, it does not help us to a more intimate apprehension of the doctrines of Lao Tzŭ than we can obtain from the isolated sayings embalmed in the writings of various philosophers and attributed by them to him. One point especially to be noticed is the persistence, even where cobwebs of mysticism hang most thickly, of the old idea of a personal if not anthropomorphic God.

At this juncture, say the first century B.C., we must temporarily take leave of Taoism. It was then, and continued to be for some time, a mixture of philosophy and superstition which interested a certain number of persons; but it was in no sense, what it came to be at a later date, a serious rival to Confucianism. The latter, meanwhile, held undisputed sway. The damage done by the Burning of the Books had been to a great extent repaired; and the Canon, with commentaries which satisfied the scholars of those days, was at the disposition of all students. But neither did the text of the Canon, still less the various commentaries, nor the doctrines as therein set forth, continue, as time went on, to satisfy everybody. Between B.C. 53 and A.D. 18 there flourished a distinguished writer, named Yang Hsiung, who, although he would have resented any attack upon his orthodoxy as a Confucianist, was nevertheless unable to accept the dogma that the nature of a man at birth is good. Neither would he follow Hsün Tzŭ and accept his conclusion that the nature of man is evil. He propounded an ethical criterion occupying a middle place between the two extremes, teaching that the nature is neither good nor evil, but a mixture of both, and that development in either direction depends wholly on environment. Subsequently, there arose what nowadays we should call a school of higher criticism. The chief exponent of this school was a scholar named Wang Ch'ung, who was born in A.D. 27. From his earliest years he showed marked signs of great literary ability. It is recorded that he used to stroll about the market-place, reading at bookstalls the books he was too poor to buy, his memory being so retentive that a single perusal was sufficient to fix the contents of a volume. After a short spell of official life, he retired dissatisfied to his home, and there composed his great work, the *Lun Hêng* or "Animadversions," in which he criticizes freely the teachings of Confucius and Mencius, and tilts generally against the errors and superstitions of his day. Once again he took up official life, but for two years only; after which he went back into private life and occupied himself with literature, chiefly of a reforming character. He memorialized the throne on the prevailing vice and extravagance; and in the days of a drunken China, he pleaded for the prohibition of alcohol; but in both cases without attracting the Emperor's attention. He was ultimately summoned to Court. The summons, however, came too late; he was already very ill, and died soon afterwards, aged about seventy. He is justly ranked as a heterodox thinker, as some extracts from his writings will speedily prove.

"The Confucianists of the present day," says Wang Ch'ung, "have great faith in their Master and accept antiquity as the standard of right. They strain every nerve to explain and practise the words which are attributed to their sages and inspired men. The writings, however, of these sages and inspired men, over which much thought and research have been spent, cannot be said to be infallibly true; how much less, then, can their casual utterances be so? But although their utterances are not true, people generally do not know how to convict them; and even if their utterances were true, because of the difficulty of grasping abstruse ideas, people generally would not know how to criticize them. I find that the words of these sages and inspired men are often contradictory, the value of one passage being frequently destroyed by the language of a later passage; but the scholars of our day do not see this. It is invariably said that the seventy disciples of Confucius were superior in talent to the Confucian scholars of to-day; but this is nonsense. According to that view, Confucius was a Master, and the inspired men who preached his doctrines must have been exceptionally gifted, and therefore different (from our scholars). The fact is that there is no difference. Those whom we now call men of genius, the ancients called inspired or divine beings; and therefore it has been said that men like the seventy disciples have rarely been heard of since that time."

The criticisms which Wang Ch'ung passes on Confucius and his teachings often seem to us trivial enough; as, for instance, when he takes exception to the language used by Confucius on finding a disciple asleep in the day-time. "Rotten wood cannot be carved," cried the angry Master; "you cannot build a wall of manure. This fellow—what is the use of my reproving him?" Wang Ch'ung thinks that sleeping in the day-time is a small fault after all, and should not entail comparison with things that are useless or loathsome. If the disciple were no better than rotten wood or manure, he should not have been admitted to an intimacy with Confucius; if, on the other hand, there was nothing else against him, then he was too harshly treated.

Wang Ch'ung is not always quite so trivial as in the above example. There is a passage in the *Lun Yü* as follows: "Confucius was expressing a wish to go and live among the nine wild tribes of the east. Someone said, 'They are uncivilized; how could you do so?' Confucius replied, 'If a superior man dwelt among them, they would not be uncivilized.'" Upon this, Wang Ch'ung remarks that Confucius was obviously dissatisfied with the progress of his doctrines in the Middle Kingdom, and therefore wanted to go away among the wild tribes. "But," he asks, "if Confucianism cannot prevail in the Middle Kingdom, how is it going to prevail among savages?" He follows this up by the use of a deadly weapon—refutation of a speaker by words from the speaker's own mouth: "Did not Confucius himself say in another passage, 'The wild tribes of the east, with their chiefs, are not equal to China with its anarchy.' And if a doctrine cannot be made to prevail where the conditions are satisfactory, how can this be effected where the conditions are unsatisfactory?"

Whatever value Wang Ch'ung's criticisms may have from the philosophic point of view, they certainly help us to realize the vigorous domination of Confucianism in the first century A.D., and the jealous guardianship which branded as a heretic anyone who disputed its authority even in the merest trifles. The Chinese have always been very tolerant of each other's religious convictions, and it was not customary in ancient China to burn persons alive for so-called errors of faith; still, at no period of Chinese history would it have been quite safe to denounce Confucius openly and in unmeasured terms as nothing better than an impostor.

Turning now to a number of passages in which Wang Ch'ung discusses the existence and attributes of a Deity, it is noticeable how often he confuses *T'ien*, God, with *t'ien*, the sky. In a few places he employs the term *Shang Ti*, and then, of course, we can only understand a personal God, a concept which, speaking generally, seems to be quite familiar to him, and for which he is directly indebted to his knowledge of the Confucian Canon. Thus, we read that *Shang Ti* granted extra years of life to a virtuous ruler; in which connexion Wang Ch'ung takes occasion to point out that the ruler in question was not particularly virtuous, and that other rulers of a more virtuous type had often died young. "There are but few good men in the empire," he goes on to argue, "and many bad ones. The good follow right principles, and the bad defy the will of God. Yet the lives of bad men are not therefore shortened, nor the lives of good men prolonged. How is it that God does not arrange that the virtuous shall always enjoy a hundred years of life, and that the wicked shall die young, as punishment for their guilt?"

There was a case of a young prince who had been unjustly done to death and whose grave had been violated. His spirit appeared to a retainer and told him that God had promised to punish the guilty one. "But God," said Wang Ch'ung, denouncing the story, "is a public Spirit. Would a public Spirit take heed of a complaint addressed to Him on a private grievance?" Other stories of alleged visits to heaven, and interviews with God (*Shang Ti*), are similarly dismissed by Wang Ch'ung as preposterous. With regard to *T'ien*, the very character for which is, as we have already seen, beyond doubt anthropomorphic, he has great difficulty in shaking himself free from the idea of "sky," in spite of numerous quotations from the Canon for which any other rendering than God would be impossible. Speaking of heaven and earth as the alleged parents of all things, he argues, to begin with, that heaven, meaning the sky, cannot possess mouth and eyes because the earth has none. Then, that heaven and earth cannot really be the authors of all creation, basing his argument upon an old story told by several other writers, as follows: "A man of the Sung State took a piece of ivory in order to carve a mulberry-leaf for his prince. He spent three years over the work, and succeeded in turning out a leaf so exact in every detail that if placed among other real mulberry-leaves no one could tell the difference. A certain philosopher, however, said, 'If God Almighty were to spend three years over every leaf, there would not be much foliage on the trees.'" On this Wang Ch'ung further enlarges: "Look at the hair and feathers of animals and birds, with their various colourings; can these have all been made? At that rate, animals and birds would never be finished. In spring we see plants growing, and in autumn we see them full-grown. Can heaven and earth have done this, or do things grow of themselves? If we say that heaven and earth have done it, they must have used hands for the purpose. Do heaven and earth possess many thousands or many myriads of hands, so that they can produce many thousands and many myriads of things, all at the same time?"

Altogether, it seems to be a mistake to regard *t'ien*, the sky, as the correlate of earth, except in the sense of ordinary phenomena. So soon as we have any expression of power, or of action, the word loses its meaning—after all, the later meaning—of sky, and reverts to what was its original meaning, God. In one remarkable passage, Wang Ch'ung introduces, simultaneously, God, *T'ien*, and God, *Shang Ti*, as though they were distinct personages, and he makes *Shang Ti* subordinate to *T'ien*. The reference is to a drought which occurred during the reign of T'ang the Completer, who came to the throne in 1766 B.C., and which had persisted for several years. The Emperor repaired alone to a grove of mulberry-trees, and having first cut off his hair and bound his hands, he offered up the following prayer: "If I alone am guilty, may my guilt not affect the welfare of the people; and if the guilt be theirs, may the punishment fall on me alone." Granting that the Emperor was in fault, Wang Ch'ung points out that "because of one man's folly, God, *T'ien*, employed God, *Shang Ti*, to injure the lives of the people." Then, because that man presented himself, with prayer, as a victim, "God, *Shang Ti*, was so pleased that rain fell at once."

Throughout his work, Wang Ch'ung sets his face steadily against all forms of supernatural intervention; he will never allow that *post hoc* is necessarily *propter hoc*. It is not surprising, therefore, to find that he adds these words: "That the Emperor personally prayed in the mulberry-grove, that his self-indictment was as mentioned, that he cut off his hair and bound his hands, thus offering himself as a victim, and that he implored God—all this may be true; but the statement that rain fell in consequence seems to be a fable. . . . It is probable that, as the drought had been lasting a long time, rain fell as a matter of course, directly after the Emperor had been accusing himself of being the cause of the drought; and that the people of that day, noticing the coincidence, thought that the rain had come in answer to prayer." Belief in divination is ridiculed by Wang Ch'ung, who argues at length to show that the will of God cannot be discovered through any arrangement of reeds or grasses or manifestations on the shell of the tortoise. His view is that people who are going to be lucky get favourable responses; those who are going to be unlucky get the reverse.

Wang Ch'ung's rather shadowy and inconsistent conception of God may be roughly summed up in a few words. He rejects anthropomorphism pure and simple: God cannot have mouth and eyes. At the same time, he gives his Deity a body and locates Him in the sky; he seems to favour the belief that the Deity lives in a palace, as a king on earth, but from this seclusion he argues that God cannot have intimate knowledge of human affairs. He does not believe that thunder is the expression of God's anger, or, indeed, that God is ever angry with mankind. "All creatures," he says, "are to God like children, and the kindness and love of father and mother are the same to all their children." But this fatherhood ceases to have significance in the face of frequent statements that God is really an immaterial fluid, which neither makes itself heard nor visible, nor does it act in any way, except as a spontaneous informing influence which ceaselessly operates throughout the universe.

If it is not easy to disentangle Wang Ch'ung's beliefs as to the existence of a God, there is no longer any difficulty when we come to the question of a world of spirits. To the old question—

> When coldness wraps this suffering clay,
> Ah, whither strays the immortal mind?

Wang Ch'ung returns a categorical answer. "The dead," he says, "do not become disembodied spirits; neither have they consciousness, nor do they injure anybody. Animals do not become spirits after death; why should man alone undergo this change? That which informs man at his birth is a vital fluid, or soul, and at death this vitality is extinguished, the body decays and becomes dust. How can it become a spirit? Vitality becomes humanity, just as water becomes ice. The ice melts and is water again; man dies and reverts to the condition of the vital fluid. Death is like the extinction of fire. When a fire is extinguished, its light does not shine any more; and when a man dies, his intellect does not perceive any more. The nature of both is the same. If people, nevertheless, pretend that the dead have knowledge, they are mistaken. The spirits which people see are invariably in the form of human beings, and that very fact is enough of itself to prove that these apparitions cannot be the souls of dead men. If a sack is filled with grain, it will stand up, and is obviously a sack of grain; but if the sack is burst and the grain falls out, then it collapses and disappears from view. Now, man's soul is enfolded in his body as grain in a sack. When the man dies, his body decays and his vitality is dissipated. When the grain is taken away, the sack loses its form; why then, when vitality is gone, should the body obtain a new shape in which to appear again in the world?

"The number of persons who have died since the world began, old, middle-aged, and young, must run into thousands of millions, far exceeding the number of persons alive at the present day. If every one of these has become a disembodied spirit, there must be at least one to every yard as we walk along the road; and those who die now must suddenly find themselves face to face with vast crowds of spirits, filling every house and street. If these spirits are the souls of dead men, they should always appear naked; for surely it is not contended that clothes have souls as well as men. It can further be shown not only that dead men never become spirits, but also that they are without consciousness, by the simple fact that before birth they are without consciousness. Before birth man rests in God; when he dies he goes back to God. God is vague and without form, and man's soul is there in a state of unconsciousness. The universe is, indeed, full of disembodied spirits, but these are not the souls of dead men. They are beings only of the mind, conjured up for the most part in sickness, when the patient is especially subject to fear. For sickness induces fear of spirits; fear of spirits causes the mind to dwell upon them; and thus apparitions are produced. Even if disembodied spirits did exist, they could not be either pleased or angry with a sacrifice, for the following reason. We must admit that spirits do not require man for their maintenance; for if they did, they would hardly be spirits. If we believe that spirits only smell the sacrifices, which sacrifices are supposed to bring either happiness or misfortune, how do we picture to ourselves the habitations of these spirits? Have they their own provisions stored up, or must they use the food of man to appease their hunger? Should they possess stores of their own, these would assuredly be other than human, and they would not have to eat human food. If they have no provisions of their own, then we should have to make offerings to them every morning and evening; and according as we sacrificed to them or did not sacrifice, they would be satiated or hungry, pleased or angry, respectively."

Wang Ch'ung's attack was directed, not only against the disembodied spirits of human beings, but against spirits of all kinds. Belief in minor deities inhabiting mountains, rivers, and trees, was shown to be absurd; the Spirit of Pestilence, and even the Spirit of Heaven, used for God in the Odes, by which term he clearly meant something more than the blue sky, were dismissed as mere figments of the imagination. "The people of to-day," he says, "rely on sacrifices. They do not improve their morals, but multiply their prayers; they do not honour their superiors, but are afraid of spirits. When they die, or when misfortune befalls them, these things are ascribed to noxious influences which have not been properly dealt with. When they have been properly dealt with, and offerings have been prepared, and yet misfortunes continue to be as numerous as before, they attribute it all to the sacrifices, declaring that they have not been performed with sufficient reverence."

At Wang Ch'ung's date, Taoism was spreading its wings. Its exponents were known, in Wang Ch'ung's words, "to vie with one another in exhibiting strange tricks and all kinds of miracles," for which no authority is to be found in any of the simple sayings of the Old Philosopher. Wang Ch'ung repeats the story—only to laugh at it—which tells how the prince of Huai-nan did finally succeed in preparing the elixir of life. Immediately on tasting the compound, he began to rise from the ground into the air; and, in his excitement, he let fall the bowl from which he had been drinking. The dogs and poultry of his establishment, running to drink up the spilt dregs, at once began to sail up after him, and the whole party was soon lost to sight in the clouds. "Exorcism," says Wang Ch'ung, "is of no use; sacrifices are of no avail. Wizards and priests have no power, for it is plain that all depends on man, and not on disembodied spirits; on his morality, and not on his sacrifices."

Wang Ch'ung has a place to himself as the first approach to a great materialistic writer. His lettered countrymen, however, do not seem to have fallen to any extent under his influence. Confucianism pursued the even tenor of its way, and Taoism continued, through the agency of magicians, charms, amulets, exorcism of evil spirits, and the like, to satisfy the craving of the masses for a supernatural element in life. Wang Ch'ung failed, for two simple reasons. His logic was in many instances anything but convincing. His attacks upon Confucius and his doctrines outraged feelings that were already deep-set. The Chinese had still to wait many centuries for a teacher who could use Confucianism as a vehicle for the conveyance of materialistic doctrines, and all to the greater glory of Confucius himself. Meanwhile, another rival was at hand.

A.D. 100-600

DURING the closing years of Wang Ch'ung's life great events were happening in China, of which he would surely have taken some notice if he had perceived their far-reaching character. Rumours of "a divine teacher in the west" had long since penetrated to China, and had been snapped up by the Taoists in a paltry forgery (*Lieh Tzŭ*, ch. iv), assigned to an imaginary philosopher of the seventh century B.C., whose alleged work can hardly be much older than the first century B.C. Now, a writer (*Shên Kua*) of the eleventh century, in a collection of miscellaneous jottings, quotes a number of historical passages to support the view that Buddhism was known in China two centuries before the Christian era; among others, the following, which was written at the close of the sixth century A.D.: "These Buddhist books had long been circulated far and wide, but disappeared with the advent of the Chin dynasty"— under which occurred the Burning of the Books (220 B.C.). With regard to the Chin dynasty, it is further on record that "in the year 216 B.C., during the reign of the so-called First Emperor, a Buddhist priest, named Shih-li-fang, and others, arrived at the capital, bringing with them, for the first time, *sûtras* written in Sanskrit." That is the historical account; a Buddhist work states that the company consisted of eighteen priests, and adds the following details: "The officials reported their arrival to the Emperor, who, on account of their strange behaviour, put them into prison. Shih-li-fang and his companions recited the *Mahâpragnâ paramitâ sûtra* (supposed to have been written by Shâkya-muni Buddha himself); whereupon a bright alight shone out and a beautiful nebula began to circle round and fill the prison. In a few moments, this revealed a golden angel, sixteen feet in height, who, majestically wielding a huge club, smashed open the prison and let the priests out (thus vividly recalling the twelfth chapter of Acts). The Emperor was terrified; and repenting his action, bestowed upon them valuable presents and sent them away." The next historical notice comes under the year 121 B.C., when we read that "for the first time an image of Buddha was secured." This is further said to have been "taken by a victorious Chinese general from a Hun chieftain, who was in the habit of worshipping it." A later history says that, "when the Emperor received the image, he had it placed in the palace among some other images, all of which averaged about ten feet in height. He did not sacrifice to it, but merely burnt incense and worshipped it with prayer. This," adds the writer, "is how Buddhism gradually began to find its way into China."

The above historical entries are generally ignored, though they have just as much claim to be recognized as the more romantic story which dates from A.D. 65. In that year we read, "The Emperor sent a mission to India, and obtained the Buddhist *Sûtra* of Forty-two Sections." The legend attached to this brief note attributes the origin of the mission to a dream in which the Emperor had a vision of a golden man with a bright halo round his head. This man, so the Emperor was told, was a Divine Being who lived in the west; and the mission was dispatched accordingly. Two years later, in A.D. 67, the mission returned, and with it came two Buddhist priests, Kâshiapmâdanga and Gobharana. They brought "The *Sûtra* of Forty-two Sections," which deals with the principles of primitive Buddhism as taught by Shâkyamuni, and which they at once set to work to translate; but before very long Kâshiapmâdanga died, leaving his colleague to carry on the task of further translation alone. Gobharana remained in China until his death at over sixty years of age; the religion, however, which he came to propagate failed to appeal closely to the Chinese imagination until several centuries had passed away. During these centuries, quite a number of other priests came to China and aided in the work of translating the Buddhist Scriptures, but it was not until A.D. 335 that the Chinese people were allowed to take Buddhist orders. This permission was due to the influence of a remarkable Indian priest, named Buddhachinga, who reached the capital in A.D. 310. He claimed supernatural powers, and pretended to foretell the future from the tinkling of bells. He could take out his viscera from a hole in his side, and wash them. He also caused a flower to bloom from an empty pot, which looks as if he combined with religion some well-known tricks of the Indian juggler.

Buddhism was now beginning to take a firm hold; and under the year 381, we read of a special temple built for priests within the Imperial palace. A further great impetus to the spread of this religion was given by the arrival, about the year 385, of Kumârajîva, a native of India who at the age of seven had been dedicated by his mother to Buddhism. His daily task was said to have been the repetition of one thousand hymns of thirty-two words to each. He devoted himself to that form of Buddhism which is known as the

Mahâyâna or Greater Vehicle, as opposed to the *Hînayâna* or Lesser Vehicle, both of them means of transporting the faithful into Nirvâna, and the latter being the older of the two. Speaking through a parable, Buddha is said to have adumbrated the wider success of the Greater Vehicle. A certain man's house took fire, whereupon he brought a goat-carriage to carry away his children. By and by, he fetched a spacious waggon. All the same, the Lesser Vehicle represents the primitive and more esoteric form of Buddhism; while the Greater Vehicle exhibits Buddha in the light of a personal Saviour, to whom intercessory prayers may be successfully offered.

Kumârajîva had taught crowds of pupils, and had preached with such success that his fame reached China, whither he was ultimately induced to proceed. There he laboured for many years as a translator, dying in 417. At death, his body was cremated; all but his tongue, which remained unhurt in the midst of the fire. The work by which he is best known, and that because of its more popular albeit abstruse character, is the translation of what is called "The Diamond *Sûtra*." This *sûtra* is especially interesting in connexion with China, as it belongs to the *Mahâyâna* school, which now prevails there and in Japan; also, because attempts have been made to show that the tenets of the *Mahâyâna* school are not purely Buddhistic, but were largely borrowed from Christianity as exhibited in the heresy of the Gnostics, with their alleged knowledge of spiritual mysteries. There are difficulties to be got over in this ascription; and it seems almost certain that the *Mahâyâna* school had already developed in western India before any knowledge of the Gospels could possibly have travelled so far. Nâgârjuna, its reputed founder, is generally assigned to the second century A.D.; and it does not appear to have been earlier than the middle of that century that the Christians at Antioch began to gather together the records of their Founder, nor indeed until the end of the second century that the Gospels became publicly known through the writings of Irenæus and Tertullian.

The Diamond *Sûtra* teaches us that all objects, all phenomena, are illusory, and have no real existence. It was delivered by the Lord Buddha to a company of twelve hundred and fifty disciples, all of whom had attained to eminent degrees of spiritual wisdom. Buddha himself had just returned from the daily quest for food, which is obtained, without solicitation, from the charitable. Having taken off his mendicant's robe, and laid aside his alms-bowl, he bathed his feet, arranged the seats, and sat down. "Then"— the following passages are translations from the Chinese text—"the venerable Subhûti, who was among the company, rose from his place; and baring his right shoulder he knelt upon his right knee, and with joined palms reverently addressed Buddha, as follows: 'O rare world-honoured One, O Tathâgata, thou who dost protect and instruct those who are Bôdhisattvas! O world-honoured One! If a good man, or a good woman, should show signs of unexcelled perfect intelligence, upon what should such a one rely, and how should such a one subdue the heart?' Buddha replied, 'Good indeed! Good indeed! As you say, I protect and instruct those who are Bôdhisattvas. Listen therefore attentively, and I will tell you.' Subhûti promptly answered that he would be glad to hear, and Buddha thereupon told the Bôdhisattvas and Mahâsattvas, as follows: 'All living creatures whatsoever, whether born from the egg, or from the womb, or from damp (as wood-lice), or by metamorphosis, whether having form or not, whether possessed of intelligence or not, whether not possessed of intelligence or not not-possessed of intelligence—all such I command to enter into the absolutely non-material state of Nirvâna, and so by extinction (of all sense-values, etc.) to obtain salvation. Thus, all living creatures will be freed from measurement, from number, and from space-limit, though in reality there are no living creatures by such extinction to obtain salvation. Why so? Subhûti, if a Bôdhisattva recognizes such objective existences as self, others, living creatures, or such a concept as old age—he is not a Bôdhisattva.'" In another passage, Buddha recurs to this theme. "A good disciple," he says, "must accustom himself to think in terms of negation as regards the existence of all living beings, whereafter it will follow that for him there will be no living beings to think about."

Section 17 of the Diamond *Sûtra* deals with the subject of faith as compared with works, and seems to show that faith in Buddha through the Buddhist Scriptures can also make a man "wise unto salvation" (2 Tim. iii. 15). It runs as follows: "O Subhûti," said Buddha, "if a good man, or a good woman, were to give up in the morning as many of his or her lives (in rebirths) as there are sands in the river Ganges, and to do the same at noonday, and again in the evening, and to continue to do this every day for an innumerable number of *kalpas*, each of an innumerable number of years; and if, on the other hand, there should be one who, having heard this *sûtra*, should yield up his heart to implicit belief—then the happiness of this last would exceed the happiness of that other. And much more would this be so if he were to write out this *sûtra*, hold fast to it himself, and recite and explain it to others. O Subhûti, let me state its importance. This sûtra has a merit which cannot be conceived of by thought, and cannot be estimated by weight or measurement." Towards the end of the *sûtra*, Buddha delivered a *gâthâ*, or stanza, referring to himself as sharing in the illusory character of all objective existences:

> If anyone sees me through the medium of form,
> Or seeks me through the medium of sound,
> Such a man is walking in a heterodox path,
> And will not be able to see the Buddha.

While Kumârajîva was spreading the faith in China, and dictating commentaries on the sacred books of Buddhism to some eight hundred priests, the famous traveller, Fa Hsien, was engaged upon his adventurous journey. On reaching manhood, he had been ordained, and subsequently proceeded to the capital to make a thorough study of the Buddhist religion. Finding that there was a lack of material for this purpose, and full of zeal and faith, he set out in A.D. 399, in company with several others, on an overland pilgrimage to India, his chief object being to obtain a complete copy of the Buddhist Canon in the original tongue. Alone of the party he reached the goal, and spent some time in India, travelling about to various important Buddhist centres and generally fulfilling the purposes of his mission. In A.D. 414 he was back in China, having returned by sea, *via* Ceylon and the Straits of Malacca, and having landed at the modern Kiaochow in Shantung. He brought with him a large number of books and sacred relics, all of which he nearly lost in the Bay of Bengal. There was a violent gale, and the ship sprang a leak. As he tells us in his own account of the journey, "he took his pitcher and ewer, with whatever else he could spare, and threw them into the sea; but he was afraid that the merchants on board would throw over his books and images, and accordingly he fixed his whole thoughts upon Kuan-shih-yin, or Kuan Yin, the Hearer of the Prayers of the World, and prayed to the sainted priests of his own country, saying, 'Oh that by your awful power you would turn back the flow of the leak and grant us to reach some resting-place!'"

Buddhism was now fairly launched, and was gaining a permanent footing in the country. We already read of Imperial devotees, and of the malign influence of priests and nuns in the palace; we also read, but need not believe, that by the year 405, nine people out of every ten had embraced the faith. Miracles of all kinds became everyday events; for instance, there was one enthusiastic priest who, in order the more effectively to impress the public, collected a number of large stones and preached to them so eloquently that they nodded as it were their heads in approval.

We have now to consider what was happening all this time to the philosophy of Lao Tzŭ, already degraded from its original speculative purity by the greed of its professional adherents, who posed as wizards and extracted money from a confiding public. The introduction of Buddhism was soon found to affect the receipts of Taoist charlatans to such an extent that something had to be done to check the ebbing tide of prosperity. A mere wizard, with a magic sword and a bundle of charms against devils and diseases, even though the people believed he could fly or render himself invisible at pleasure, had no chance with a Buddhist priest, his temple, his ritual, and his promise of a salvation, understood by the Chinese in the sense of an immortality of happiness after death. Therefore, in order to compete for public favour upon more equal terms, the Taoists transformed what had once been a philosophic cult into an actual religion, by the simple process of borrowing. We have already noticed an attempt to show that the *Mahâyâna*, or Greater Vehicle, was derived through the Gnostics from Christianity; it is a much easier matter to prove that Taoism, as a religion, is little more than Buddhism under another name. The Taoists took over, almost en bloc, the ceremonial of the Buddhists, much of which bears an extraordinary resemblance to the ceremonial of the Roman Catholic Church, though it can hardly, in view of the relative dates, be said to have been borrowed therefrom; any borrowing must have been the other way round.

One of the earliest formulas adopted by devout Buddhists, practically amounting to a creed, was the following statement of faith: "I put my trust in the Lord Buddha; I put my trust in his Law; I put my trust in his Church." The *Mahâyâna* school based upon that creed the doctrine of a Trinity—Buddha, his Law, and his Church, popularly known as the Three Preciosities; and this trio has been further explained as a Trinity in Unity (see Lecture VIII), the transcendency of which is not in the least appreciated or understood by the people at large, who regard the three representative images to be found in Buddhist temples as three separate deities, to be conciliated by prayer and offerings.

Buddhism has covered China with monasteries, nunneries, and shrines of varying size and importance. The priests and nuns take vows of celibacy, and of abstinence from flesh and wine; they shave their heads; they fast, even on a vegetable diet; they sit daily in meditation. Among other striking features of Buddhism as seen in China, such as have suggested a common source with Christian worship, if not actual borrowing by one religion from the other, may be mentioned the liturgies chanted by the priests, vestments, midnight masses, prayers for the dead, altars decorated with flowers and candles, bowls of water as the emblem of purity set forth in the life and teachings of the Buddha; and the use of incense, practised, however, before Buddhism was heard of. On the other hand, there is the ever-recurring statue of Kuan Yin, to whom we have seen that Fa Hsien prayed in his distress; originally an incarnation of Buddha, and represented down to the early part of the twelfth century as a man, but now as a woman holding a baby, the two bearing a remarkable resemblance to our own pictures of the Virgin and Child, of which the Chinese figures are thought by some to be a late copy.

The copying we have now to consider is that of Taoism in regard to the instrumental parts of the Buddhist religion. In a word, the Taoists may be said to have copied almost all the above characteristics of Buddhism. They built temples and monasteries, and even provided a Trinity, consisting of Lao Tzǔ, P'an Ku, and God, but stopping short of any suggestion of Unity. P'an Ku was the first being brought into existence by cosmogonical evolution. He is said to have sprung into life fully endowed with perfect knowledge, and his function was to set the economy of the universe in order. He is often depicted as wielding a huge adze, and engaged in fashioning the world. With his death the details of creation began. His breath became the wind; his voice, the thunder; his left eye, the sun; his right eye, the moon; his blood formed rivers; his hair grew into trees and plants; his flesh became the soil; his sweat descended as rain; and the parasites which infested his body were the origin of the human race. Such was the second person of the Taoist Trinity. The name of the third is made up of *Yü huang* = Jade Ruler, and *Shang Ti*, which is already familiar to us as an alternative for *T'ien* = God. By the images of their Trinity, a Taoist temple is readily distinguished from a Buddhist temple; there are, of course, various other characteristics of the two places of worship, but they are not so obvious to the uninitiated. A Taoist priest does not shave the whole head; and formerly he was allowed to marry, but since the tenth century celibacy has been strictly enforced.

With the annexation by the Taoists of all the more attractive and also minatory features of Buddhism, such as a heaven for the good and a hell for the wicked, there began a long struggle for supremacy which lasted through many centuries before the two faiths—Taoism having become a religion—could agree to work side by side, as they do now, without interfering one with the other. Sometimes Taoism flourished, under the influence of Court favour; at other times, Buddhism would be all the rage, with Emperor and Empress as its most earnest devotees. One of the great poets of the fifth century wrote an elaborate eulogy of Buddhism, perhaps the first of its kind. A statesman and scholar of the same period objected to Taoism as opposed to the ordinary instincts of humanity; but he hated Buddhism still more, chiefly because of its foreign origin. In A.D. 446 he discovered a secret store of arms in a Buddhist temple, in consequence of which many of the priests were put to death, their books and images destroyed, and for a time the practice of this religion was prohibited. The catastrophe would have been greater but for the action of the heir-apparent, a devout Buddhist, who gave the priests warning of their danger. The statesman himself was converted to Taoism by a priest who pretended to have received a revelation from Lao Tzǔ; the priest was appointed to be the Pope of the Taoist church, and a magnificent temple was built for his reception.

The institution of the Taoist Papacy—to use a convenient term—is claimed for the first century A.D. There was at that date a precocious child, named Chang Tao-ling, who is said to have mastered the philosophy of Lao Tzǔ by the time he was seven years old. Declining to take office, he retired to the mountains and devoted himself to the study of alchemy. On one occasion, he went to the province of Ssǔch'uan to drive out troublesome demons, which he would better have accomplished, according to Lao Tzǔ, by staying at home and doing nothing. An individual of the same surname, who traces his descent from this Chang Tao-ling, still holds the title of Pope; and it has certainly been so held for many centuries, even if it does not go so far back as is claimed. The functions of the modern Pope are chiefly confined to blessing and selling charms and amulets, to be used against, disease and similar machinations of evil spirits. It has never, however, been this aspect of Taoism which has influenced statesmen and inspired poets. Taoism has always, since its early degradation, existed under two forms. There is the Taoism of superstition, with its grafts from Buddhism, for the masses; and there is the Taoism of speculation and paradox for the cultured, though sometimes the cultured are even more under the influence of superstition than are the masses.

In the year A.D. 471 the Emperor under the Northern Wei dynasty—China was then divided—resigned his throne and devoted himself to Taoism. In the same year the Emperor of the Liu Sung dynasty spent vast sums in building a Buddhist monastery, and boasted that he was laying up merit for himself in the next world. A minister is said to have remonstrated, showing that the people had sold wives and children in order to meet the charges laid on them, and asking where merit could lie; upon which, the Emperor repented and caused the monastery to be pulled down. In the year 484 an Imperial prince of the Southern Ch'i dynasty became an ardent supporter of Buddhism, and surrounded himself with priests in great numbers. A learned official endeavoured to persuade him that the whole scheme of Buddhism was a sham. He argued that Buddha having died, his spirit could no longer be in existence, spirit being to the body what sharpness is to a knife; when the knife goes, its sharpness goes with it. Another official told his wife, who was a firm believer, that he was going to write an essay proving that there was no such being as Buddha. "If there is no such being as Buddha," rejoined the lady, tartly, "why write an essay about him?"

We left Confucianism at the close of the first century, battered but not bruised by the attacks of Wang Ch'ung. Taoism was then still more or less a philosophic cult; Buddhism had as yet made no advance. The birthplace of Confucius had become a goal for the Confucian pilgrim; a shrine had been built there, and even Emperors found their way thither, to do honour to the great Teacher. One of the latter had visited the spot so early as A.D. 72, and after worshipping Confucius, coupled with his seventy-two disciples, gave orders that the heir-apparent and all the Court should devote themselves to a study of the Confucian Canon. Under the reign of the Emperor Ming Ti, A.D. 227-239, there is an echo of Confucianism, from its religious side, in an edict which was published after an eclipse of the sun in A.D. 233, in order to restore public confidence. "We have heard," says the Emperor, "that if a sovereign is remiss in government, God terrifies him by calamities and portents. These are divine reprimands sent to recall him to a sense of duty. Thus, eclipses of the sun and moon are manifest warnings that the rod of empire is not wielded aright. Ever since We ascended the throne, Our inability to continue the glorious traditions of Our departed ancestors and carry on the great work of civilization has now culminated in a warning message from on high. It therefore behoves Us to issue commands for personal reformation, in order to avert impending calamity. The relationship, however, between God and man is that of father and son; and a father, about to chastise his son, would not be deterred were the latter to present him with a dish of meat. We do not therefore consider it a part of Our duty to act in accordance with certain memorials advising that the Grand Astrologer be instructed to offer up sacrifices on this occasion. Do ye governors of districts, and other high officers of State, seek rather to rectify your own hearts; and if anyone can devise means to make up for Our shortcomings, let him submit his proposals to the throne."

The enlightened Emperor who penned these lines was ruler of one of the Three Kingdoms, founded by his grandfather, Ts'ao Ts'ao, the famous general, who, like many other founders of houses in China, never mounted the throne. The grandson was a handsome man, and when he stood up his beard touched the ground; but he is interesting to us for a very different reason. Under his reign, women were for the first time admitted to official life, and several actually rose to important posts. The experiment was tried again in the eighth century, but was soon given up. His father, who was the first actual sovereign of the dynasty, was an ardent Taoist. He used to preach to his Court on the doctrines of Lao Tzŭ, and always became very angry with any official who either stretched himself, yawned, or expectorated. At the same time, he was careful to see that the Confucian shrine, which showed signs of decay, was put into proper repair. Throughout the long history of China it is noticeable that Confucianism, though faced by more attractive rivals, never quite loses its hold. Many Emperors indulged freely in heterodox teachings, so far as their more private life was concerned; but except in one notable instance, to which we shall come by and by, they seem to have felt that Confucius had a backing of the nation's intellect and scholarship which it would not do to ignore.

In A.D. 505 the first Confucian temple, as we now understand the term, was built and dedicated. Images of Confucius were then introduced into the temple, some say for the first time; others hold that in A.D. 178 a likeness of Confucius had been placed in his shrine, as a substitute for the wooden tablet in use up to that date. Although it is correct to distinguish between the earlier shrine and the more elaborate temple which we are now about to consider, there is no doubt that the shrine played an important part in keeping alive the Confucian tradition. So far back as A.D. 267, an Emperor decreed that the sacrifice of a pig, a sheep, and an ox should be offered to Confucius at each of the four seasons. Rules were also drawn up about A.D. 430 for regulating the ceremonies to be performed. Gradually, the people came to look upon Confucius as a god to be propitiated for the sake of worldly advantages; and in A.D. 472 it became necessary to issue an edict forbidding women to frequent the shrine for the purpose of praying for children.

About A.D. 555 it was enacted that a Confucian temple should be built in every prefectural city in the empire. Various changes were made from time to time in the internal arrangements of the building. Some of the ancient sages who were admitted to share in the honours accorded to their Master, appeared in the shape of wooden figures; the portraits of others were painted on the walls. In the year 960 the wooden figures were abolished, and clay images were substituted. These were in turn replaced, in the year 1530, by simple wooden tablets. At another period, the numbers of the musicians and dancers were altered; and so on. It will here be convenient, perhaps, to bring the story of the Confucian temple, with all its important bearings upon national life and religion, down to the present day.

In the early shrines, the only image was that of Confucius; but when the order was given for the general erection of Confucian temples, that of Yen Hui was added. He was emphatically the disciple whom Confucius loved. He would listen with what appeared to be stolid indifference to his Master's teachings, and then he would go away and strive to put into practice the principles he had learned. He is still affectionately remembered by his countrymen, although Ssŭ-ma Ch'ien, the historian, attributes his splendid reputation chiefly to his close connexion with Confucius, quaintly likening him to a fly which travels far and fast by clinging to the tail of a courser. By degrees, batches of disciples and other worthies were admitted to the honours of the temple, until the number of tablets was considerably enlarged. The first Manchu Emperors, who were throughout among the warmest supporters of Confucianism, made it their business to see that a temple was established in every prefecture, district city, and market town all over the empire. The tablets were rearranged, and a revised ceremonial was introduced. At the present day, we find the tablet of Confucius in a hall at the north end of the temple, facing south. It had always been placed on the east side down to the eighth century, the south-facing position being that of an Emperor on his throne; but from that date Confucius was recognized as the peer of Emperors. To the right and left of his tablet are the tablets of the Four Associates, of whom Yen Hui is the first and Mencius is the fourth. The second and third are, respectively, Tsêng Ts'an, the author of the "Classic of Filial Piety" and reputed author of the "Great Learning," one of the Four Books, and Tzŭ Ssŭ, the grandson of Confucius, author of the "Doctrine of the Mean," which, with the Confucian Analects and the works of Mencius, completes the tale of the Four Books, the first division of the Confucian Canon. Then come the tablets of the Twelve Sages, which number might have for us a suggestive ring, particularly when taken in conjunction with the Four Associates. Unfortunately for those who love to draw hasty parallels, of the Four Associates only three could possibly be regarded as Evangelists in the sense of spreading the Gospel by their writings; and of the Twelve Sages only eleven had actually been intimate disciples, the twelfth being the philosopher Chu Fu Tzŭ, of the twelfth century A.D.

Besides the above, space has to be allotted to the tablets of the ancestors of Confucius for five generations; also for the tablets of seventy-nine of the most prominent worthies of past ages, including all other known disciples of Confucius beyond those already mentioned. Then comes a contingent of sixty to seventy tablets, representing great Confucian scholars of all dynasties, every one of whom, as a condition of admission, must have contributed largely to the elucidation and support of Confucian doctrine. Altogether, there are about one hundred and seventy tablets, inscribed with the name of each individual and his rank in the temple. Admission to the national Walhalla, the honour of which has always been much coveted by the families of deceased Confucianists, does not always confer that permanent place with posterity which it might be supposed would be the case. The Chinese, always noted for an especially practical turn of mind, have reserved to themselves the right to revise the decisions of their ancestors in regard to the merit of all those whose tablets stand in the temple. They feel that a popular impulse, justifiable at the moment, a personal intrigue, or Court favour, may sometimes have succeeded in giving a man more than was his due; it then remains to secure the removal of such a tablet, and to substitute that of a worthier representative. A tablet, however, which has once been removed is under no disability; it may be restored at a later date. This perhaps is the least satisfactory feature of all, aggravating rather than otherwise the instability of the institution. For instance, a Confucianist, named Fan Ning, was ranked in A.D. 647 among the Associates, but under the next reign he was reduced to the position of Scholar. In 1530 his tablet was removed from the temple; in 1724 it was replaced. Still, there are many instances in which the prerogative has been justly used; and it seems desirable that before very long some such system should be tentatively applied to the monuments in Westminster Abbey and other injudiciously crowded shrines.

The worship in the Confucian temple is celebrated twice a year, in spring and in autumn. In the provinces, the official who performs the ceremony is the chief civil authority. He is accompanied by the general body of civil and military officers, by a band of musicians, and by thirty-six dancers. On the morning of the worship, the tables and altars are covered with offerings which have been prepared the day before. In front of the tablet of Confucius is an altar on which stand an incense-burner and two large lighted candles. A table before this altar is spread with bowls of grain, cups of wine, etc.; and on the east and west sides are tables furnished with vessels containing various articles of food. In the middle of the hall a roll of white silk is laid out, and before it are the three victims, an ox, with a sheep on one side and a pig on the other. Similar offerings, but fewer in number and in all cases without the ox, are set out in front of the other tablets. The official who is to preside as chief worshipper is supposed to have fasted and purified himself by ablution during the three preceding days. He arrives at the temple before daylight, and assumes his Court dress. Under the guidance of the master of the ceremonies, he takes up a position at the head of his civilian colleagues on the east side of the hall, the military officials being stationed on the west side. The service begins with music and a hymn, after which the chief worshipper ascends to the tablet of Confucius, where he kneels, strikes the ground with his head, and offers incense on the altar. He then resumes his place, but only to ascend and descend twice more with the same ceremonial. During the intervals there is music, and dancers perform slow-time and dignified evolutions. The spirit of Confucius is supposed to arrive and take part in the ceremony so soon as the music begins. The first hymn is called "Receiving the Spirit," and is sung very slowly and reverently, as befitting such a tremendous occasion.

> Mighty art thou, O Confucius,
> Perceiver of the future, endowed with foreknowledge,
> Compeer of God our father, and of Earth our mother,
> Teacher of the myriad ages,
> Auspicious fulfilment of the skein on the *lin*,
> Thy voice has a music of metal and silk,
> By thy aid the sun and moon run their courses,
> And the stability of the universe is preserved.

The *lin* is a fabulous animal which appeared to the mother of Confucius before the latter's birth. She tied a skein of silk round its horn; and when, just before the death of Confucius, the animal appeared again, the skein was still attached to the horn. This was the "fulfilment" mentioned in the hymn.

By the second century B.C. the old music, of which Confucius speaks, was gone, and had been replaced by a system brought from the Greek kingdom of Bactria about the year 126 B.C. The music of the Confucian age, scores and instruments alike, perished at the Burning of the Books, and we read that in the first part of the second century B.C. the hereditary Grand Music-Master was altogether ignorant of his art. The extraordinary similarities between the Chinese and Pythagorean systems of music place it beyond a doubt that one must have been derived from the other. The early Jesuit fathers declared that the ancient Greeks borrowed their music from the Chinese; but we know that the music in question did not exist in China until two centuries after its appearance in Greece.

As to the dances, the movements of which are very like those of the minuet, they seem to be of purely native origin. In the commentary to the History of the Later Han dynasty, which covered the first two centuries of the Christian era, we are told that "the origin of these dances is not known, but that they were formerly used in the worship of God." The dance is essentially a step-dance, and not mere posturing as some have thought; it may be compared with the Greek ὄρχησις, which was not only rhythmical but also pantomimic in character, though there is no suggestion that these dances came with the music from Greece. The ancient official dance of China was performed altogether without accessories. A short poem of perhaps sixteen words having been chosen, two performers, dressed in the now old-fashioned robe of the graduate and accompanied by music, would proceed to illustrate these words, expressing each individual word by a figure (as in a quadrille) of eight separate movements. Thus, the number of figures to a dance would depend upon the number of words in the poem. The dances are usually performed, at the present day, by eight pairs of dancers, each of whom holds in his left hand a flute, and in his right hand a triple pheasant's feather. This arrangement was supposed to be in accordance with a verse in the Odes; but, unfortunately, it is now certain that the word which has been understood to mean "pheasant's feather" really means "flute." Thus, instead of having a flute in one hand and in the other a feather, the latter of which would effectually prevent the dancer from playing upon the former, we find that the dancer was really provided with a flute for each hand; in other words, a double flute like that of the

Greeks, which was played with both hands, the treble half being held in the left hand, the bass in the right.

Such is the Confucian temple, the worship in which has been conducted upon much the same lines for the past fourteen hundred years. An inner meaning is attributed to the various accessories at which we have merely glanced. The roll of white silk is an emblem of purity; the ox, of stability; the pig, of determination—a symbolism gathered somehow from its bristles; the sheep represents food and clothing; and the incense suggests virtue, fragrance being always associated with good deeds and a good reputation. The composition of the sacrifice—an ox between a sheep and a pig—is noteworthy, if nothing more, for its identity with the *suovetaurilia* of the Romans, a sacrifice offered at lustrations.

We left Buddhism and Taoism, both flourishing, in the fifth and sixth centuries, and now, before picking up again the chronological thread, it will be convenient to introduce brief notices of several foreign religions, the majority of which enjoyed but a meteor-like existence, leaving only one to survive to the present day. The first of these was the religion of Zoroaster, whose idea of the resurrection glorified man's body as his eternal companion. It is known as Mazdaism, and was imported from Persia into China towards the close of the sixth or beginning of the seventh century. As a term for God, the early Mazdæans adopted a character, pronounced *Hsien*, already in use in China with that same signification. They were permitted to build temples, and these are mentioned in Chinese records as having been erected at the capital during the seventh century. The Chinese, however, do not seem to have been much attracted by fire-worship; and, moreover, it was not long before there were two other rivals in the field.

The Christian schism of Manichæus, which had once been a form of faith dear to St Augustine, enjoyed perhaps a better chance than Mazdaism. Its dualistic theology, in which Satan is represented as co-eternal with God, bore at least sufficient resemblance to the dual system of the positive and negative principles to arrest the attention of the Chinese; and this resemblance seems to have been exploited by the Manichæan missionaries, who preached in China during the seventh century, and during the eighth century had temples at several important centres of population, but were finally suppressed in 843. Our interest in Manichæism has been greatly stimulated in recent days by the discovery of a Manichæan treatise in Chinese, unfortunately of uncertain date. This document was brought by

Professor Pelliot from the Caves of the Thousand Buddhas at Tun-huang, in the province of Kansuh, where it had been bricked up for many centuries. From it we gain some interesting information. Not only is it like in form to a Buddhist *sûtra*, but it is tinged here and there with traces of Buddhist thought, reminding us how the Buddhists themselves, when they first sought to convert Japan, were careful to begin by canonizing various Shinto or native gods, in order to impart an air of familiarity to the new religion. Taoist influence may also be traced. The opening words, but apparently not very many of them, are lost; we start, however, with a complete question put by a personage who has been identified with Addas, mentioned in the *Acta Archelai* as the apostle of Manichæism in the East, and answered by Manichæus himself. "Is the original nature of the carnal body," asks Addas, "single or double?" By "double" the questioner seems to refer to the subdivision of the soul into light and dark, the dualism which I have just said was part of the Manichæan system. To this, Manichæus, here called the Envoy of Light, began his reply in the very words of Buddha in the Diamond *Sûtra*, the Chinese characters being the same in both cases, "Good indeed! Good indeed! In order to benefit the innumerable crowds of living beings, you have addressed to me this query, profound and mysterious. You thus show yourself a good friend to all those living beings of the world who have blindly gone astray, and I will now explain the matter to you in detail, so that the net of doubt in which you are ensnared may be broken for ever without recall. Know, then, that before this world was created, two Envoys of Light, namely, the Holy Ghost and the Good Mother of Life, entered into the dark abyss of the sunless land, from which they returned victorious, clad in the cuirass of knowledge of the five divisions of bright bodies (the five elements), which they skilfully used to help themselves to get out of the five abysses. The five classes of demons clung to the five elements, as flies cling to honey, like birds caught by bird-lime, or like fishes which have swallowed the hook. Therefore, the Holy Ghost, the Envoy of Light, took the five classes of demons and the five elements, and combining the powers of these in due relation one to the other, made the ten heavens and eight earths of the universe. Thus, the universe is, for the five elements, a druggery where they may be cured, and for the demons, a prison where they may be kept under restraint."

Manichæus goes on to show that the five elements became, as it were, the prison in which the demons were confined—good and evil in a state of almost chemical union, wherein the traces of each component part are obliterated. The governors of the prison are the five sons of the Holy Ghost, who are expressed by such abstractions as cogitation, intelligence, reflection, thought, arid apprehension. Satan then comes upon the scene; and "when he saw these things, he once more conceived in his poisonous heart a wicked scheme. He ordered two demons, a male and a female, to take upon themselves the likenesses of the Holy Ghost and of the Good Mother, and then to create by magic the body of a man, in imitation of the material universe. Thus, the carnal body, tainted with the poison of evil passions, although on a tiny scale, yet reproduced in itself every single feature of heaven and earth. . . . Just as when a goldsmith copies the form of an elephant, drawing it inside a finger-ring, and neither adding to it nor taking away from it, so was man made in the exact likeness of the universe." Further, in revenge for the treatment of the demons by the Holy Ghost, Satan conceived another wicked and poisonous plan. He shut up the five bright natures in the carnal body, of which he fashioned a small universe, and so put an end to their independence of action. He also planted five trees of death, in order to disturb as much as possible the original human nature. "Thus, the tree of dark cogitation springs up within the barrier of the bones; its fruit is resentment. The tree of dark intelligence springs up within the barrier of the muscles; its fruit is anger. The tree of dark reflection springs up within the barrier of the veins; its fruit is licentiousness. The tree of dark thought springs up within the barrier of the flesh; its fruit is rage. The tree of dark apprehension springs up within the barrier of the skin; its fruit is folly."

Again, we read that "the Holy Ghost had constructed two bright ships to transport good men over the sea of life and death, back to their original home (with God), so that their brilliantly lighted natures should find peace and happiness at last. When Satan saw this, his mind was at once filled with anger and jealousy; and he proceeded to make two forms, one male and the other female, after the fashion of the two great bright ships which are the sun and moon, in order to introduce disturbance and confusion into the bright nature of man." The two forms thus constructed by Satan became, as it were, two dark ships, in contrast with the bright ships of the Holy Ghost, and carried their freight of bright human nature into hell, where all sorts of torments were suffered, and from which it was difficult to obtain deliverance. Then, when there comes into the world some Envoy of Light, such as one of the predecessors of Manichæus, who desires to instruct and reform mankind, in order to deliver them from suffering, he begins, we are told, "by causing the sound of the beautiful Word to pass through the portal of the ear; after which he enters into the abodes of false religions, [1] and, relying upon the virtue of spiritual invocation, chains up the crowd of venomous serpents and evil beasts, and no more allows them independence and freedom. Further, armed with the axe of wisdom, he cuts down the poisonous trees, tearing up their very roots, together with all kinds of foul vegetation."

Enough has been said, perhaps, to give an idea of the shape in which Manichæan Christianity was presented to the Chinese people, often confused by them with Mazdaism, the fire-worshipping religion of Zoroaster. As has been already stated, we do not possess the opening words of this treatise, and cannot therefore say if they coincide with the conventional words with which a Buddhist *sûtra* begins; but we may fairly infer that such was the case, partly from the remarkable imitation of Buddhist phraseology throughout, and also from the closing sentence, the Chinese text of which, *mutatis mutandis*, might well be interchanged with that of the Diamond Sûtra:

Diamond Sûtra	*Manichæan Treatise*
When Buddha had delivered this *sûtra*, all the monks and nuns, lay-brothers and lay-sisters, together with all the *dêvas* and demons in the universe, having heard Buddha's words, rejoiced with one accord, and accepting them with faith, proceeded to put them into practice.	Then, all the members of the great assembly, having heard this *sûtra*, accepted it with faith and rejoicing, and proceeded to put it into practice.

---

[1] Kindly suggested by Prof. A. A. Bevan.

A.D. 600-1000

WHILE the Manichæans were endeavouring to spread among the Chinese what can only be called a travesty of Christian doctrine, another sect from the west, heterodox indeed, but not egregiously so, came to offer a new creed. The followers of Nestorius, the famous patriarch at Constantinople in the fifth century, the chief flaw in whose teaching was that he held Christ to have had distinct human and divine persons, dispatched a mission which reached China in A.D. 631, and introduced into China what is now known as Nestorian Christianity, under the title of the Luminous Doctrine. By the year 635 this religion had made such headway that its missionaries were allowed to settle at Chang-an, the capital. In 638 the first Christian church was built there, and the following Imperial decree was issued: "The TRUTH does not always appear under the same name, nor is divine inspiration always embodied in the same form. Religions vary in various lands, but the underlying principle of all is the salvation of mankind"—a very remarkable admission by a Chinese Emperor of the seventh century that there is "truth" outside Confucianism, and that there are other prophets besides Confucius. To continue with the decree: "The Persian priest Raban (really a Syrian) has come from afar, bringing with him sacred books and a doctrine which he has submitted to Us at the capital. Carefully examining the object of this doctrine, We find that it is profoundly mysterious and associated with inaction (Lao Tzŭ's great principle); it establishes the important points of our birth and growth; it helps animals and it profits mankind; and therefore it should circulate wherever in the world We hold sway. Let a monastery be founded in the I-ning ward of Our capital, and let twenty-one priests be appointed to serve it."

Under such auspices, it is not surprising that the Luminous Doctrine continued to flourish, as flourish it must have done for some centuries. Marco Polo mentions Nestorianism as still in existence during the thirteenth century. He meets with it, on his long journeys, in many places, and also mentions it in connexion with the camp of Genghis Khan, marching against Prester John, who was at that date supposed to be a king somewhere in Central Asia. He tells us that Genghis "one day summoned before him his astrologers, both Christians and Saracens, and desired them to let him know which of the two hosts would gain the battle, his own or Prester John's. The Saracens tried to ascertain, but were unable to give a true answer; the Christians, however, did give a true answer, and showed manifestly before him how the event should be. For they got a cane and split it lengthwise, and laid one half on this side and one half on that, allowing no one to touch the pieces. And one piece of cane they called Genghis Khan, and the other piece they called Prester John. And then they said to Genghis: 'Now mark! and you will see the event of the battle, and who shall have the best of it; for whose cane shall get above the other, to him shall victory be.' Genghis replied that he would fain see it, and bade them begin. Then the Christian astrologers read a psalm out of the Psalter, and went through other incantations. And lo! whilst all were beholding, the cane that bore the name of Genghis Khan, without being touched by anybody, advanced to the other that bore the name of Prester John, and got on the top of it. When Genghis saw that, he was greatly delighted, and seeing how in this matter he found the Christians to tell the truth, he always treated them with great respect, and held them for men of truth ever after."

Marco Polo finds "a few Nestorian Christians" in Yunnan, who "never eat wheaten bread because in that country it is unwholesome. Rice they eat, and make of it sundry messes, besides a kind of drink which is very clear and good, and makes a man drunk, just as wine does." In Ho-kien Fu, Chihli, he finds "certain Christians, who have a church," and of Hangchow he says, "There is one church only, belonging to the Nestorian Christians." Of Chinkiang Fu he says, "There are in this city two churches of Nestorian Christians, which were established in the year of our Lord 1278;" and he goes on to explain that Kublai Khan, then Emperor of China, had appointed "a Nestorian Christian to be governor of that city for three years, during which he caused two Christian churches to be built, and since then there they are. But before his time there was no church, neither were there any Christians."

During the fourteenth century Nestorianism seems to have faded away, and but for a lucky accident, our knowledge of its appearance in China would have been scanty indeed. For reasons that we shall come to later on, the appeal of Christianity to the Chinese has never had a chance against the appeal of Buddhism; nor even against the appeal of Mahometanism; and Chinese literature has been ransacked in vain to discover any traces of the comparatively long stay of the great faith which by Marco Polo's time had taken such deep root in the west. However, in 1625 some workmen, in the course of certain excavations at a town about forty miles from Hsi-an Fu, in the province of Shensi, came across a large inscribed tablet of stone, about nine feet in height, which at once attracted the attention of the local authorities, who caused it to be removed to a temple about a mile or so outside Hsi-an Fu. The tablet soon became an object of interest to native archæologists, and much more so to foreign archæologists, so soon as, through the medium of the Jesuit fathers, its existence and its inscription had been revealed to western scholars. For the inscription was nothing less than a general account in Chinese of the Christian religion and of its establishment in China, running to a total of two thousand and thirty-six characters, or nearly the equivalent of three thousand words in English, and followed by a short inscription and a list of names in Syriac. The genuineness of this tablet was not allowed to pass without question. Among the names of distinguished persons who refused, and with some justification, to accept the stone as a true witness, were those of Voltaire, and (later) Neumann, Renan, and Stanislas Julien, of whom the two last-mentioned ultimately saw good reasons for changing their opinions. At the present day, there is no longer any doubt about the genuineness of the tablet. Its value, indeed, has been so far recognized by western collectors that in 1907 an attempt was made to carry it off bodily. Happily, the attempt was foiled, and the tablet was removed to a position of greater safety.

It may be interesting now to touch briefly on the tenor of this inscription, forming, as it does, a striking contrast with the presentation of Christianity as gathered from the Manichæan treatise. The opening paragraph is an adoration of the Triune God, followed up by an account of the creation of the universe, and of man in a state of moral perfection. Grafted, however, on to such details as are more or less in harmony with the first chapter of Genesis, we find an item which belongs to purely Chinese cosmogony: "God excited (as by a drum) the primeval spirit, and called into being the two breaths (or influences)," alluding to the Yin and the Yang, the passive and active principles, by the interaction of which, according to the Chinese view, all things were, and are still being produced. The introduction of this sentence, not to mention others, which must be regarded as conciliatory, if not *ad captandum*, militates somewhat against a theory which has been propounded, namely, that the stone was miraculously preserved, and is an answer to the taunt that "God had left the Middle Kingdom for more than fifteen hundred years (*i.e.* up to the arrival of Catholic missionaries in the sixteenth century) without a word of the only Name under heaven whereby men must be saved" (Rev. A. C. Moule, *Journal of C.B.R.A.S.*, vol. xli. p. 77). Further, the phraseology is often either Buddhistic or Taoistic, although recognized classical expressions from the Canon do predominate. The Jesuit father, P. Havret, made a calculation that out of three hundred to four hundred quotations or allusions appearing on the tablet, about two hundred and fifty came from the Confucian Canon and the standard histories; so that in point of view of style, the tablet is so far strongly fortified.

The next item recorded in the inscription is the appearance of Satan, who, under the guise of innocence, destroyed man's original pure nature, leading, we are told, to the rapid formation of three hundred and sixty-five heretical sects, as though one for each day in the year. "Some of these," in the words of the inscription, "took material objects as their gods; others (meaning the Buddhists) maintained the illusory nature of all things, and were swept into devious paths; others again trusted for happiness to prayer and sacrifice; and again others made a display of virtue in order to impose upon the world. Wise concern for the future was lost in the confusion; all feelings were worn out; and all was vague without attainment. The fire that oppressed men became a scorching flame; amid the encircling gloom they lost their way; and after long wanderings they failed to return. At this juncture, the Triune God became One; and the luminous and venerable Messiah, gathering Himself under a disguise of His real majesty, came forth among the generations of men. Spirits and *dêvas* (a Buddhist phrase, probably used here as the best equivalent for angels) proclaimed with joy that a virgin had given birth to the Holy One in Syria. A bright star announced the auspicious event, and Persians, seeing its brilliant light, came to bring tribute. Thus He fulfilled the prophecies in the books of the Old Testament, and with supreme wisdom arranged the management of the family and of the State (these last phrases are based upon 'The Great Learning,' one of the Four Books). He established the new doctrine, which cannot be expressed in words, of the Triune Holy Ghost (apropos of which, it will be remembered, that the *Tao* of Lao Tzŭ 'cannot be expressed in words'). He made good works subordinate to faith (as Buddha did in the Diamond *Sûtra*). He enunciated the Eight States (or conditions, for which non-Chinese term, possibly Buddhist, it has been suggested that we should understand the Beatitudes), that worldliness might be refined away, and purity achieved. He opened a door for the three Constant Practices (a classical term, meaning (1) the appointment of wise men by the sovereign, (2) the reliance on wise men by the officials, and (3) the respect for wise men by the people)." This last seems to be a singular item, so much so that Dr Legge suggested the Three Graces—faith, hope, and charity; but the phrase belongs to Chinese literature, as here translated. Mr A. C. Moule, following Havret, gives, "He revealed the gates of the three which abide," without any hint as to who or what the three are. To proceed: "He established life and abolished death. He was hung up like a luminous sun, in order to prevail against the gates of hell, and thus the wiles of Satan were wholly frustrated." Mr A. Wylie translates, "He suspended the bright sun;" Dr Legge has, "He hung up the bright sun;" and Mr Moule, following Père Havret, has, "He hung up a bright sun"—all of which are without meaning. The allusion is obviously to Christ's death on the cross: "A light to lighten the Gentiles." To continue: "He rowed the boat of mercy, in order to reach the bright palace; and in it souls are conveyed thither. His great work being now done, He ascended to heaven at noon of the day." What authority the Nestorians had for placing the Ascension at noon it is difficult to say; so far as can be gathered from the divergent accounts in the New Testament, the hour would seem to have been a late one in the evening.

We need not go further into the language of this inscription, which from this point onwards is chiefly laudatory of those Emperors of the T'ang dynasty who were favourable to, or at any rate tolerant of, the faith: T'ai Tsung, who in 638 had issued the decree already quoted; Kao Tsung, his son, who founded Christian monasteries, but fell under the influence of the terrible Empress Wu, a fanatical Buddhist and therefore an oppressor of the Nestorians; the famous Ming Huang, who ordered the wrecked Nestorian temples to be rebuilt, and sent the portraits of his five Imperial ancestors to be hung in the monastery at the capital; Su Tsung, who also rebuilt monasteries, and generally patronized the faith; Tai Tsung, who annually on his own birthday (not on the day of the Nativity, as some have thought) sent a present of incense and food from the Imperial table, in honour of the church; and finally, the then reigning Emperor, posthumously known as Tê Tsung. These bring us down to 781, the year in which the tablet was set up. From this enumeration of Emperors and their attitude to Nestorianism, one fact stands out clearly: that Christianity had already enjoyed for one hundred and fifty years a meed not merely of tolerance, but of actual patronage in high quarters, which has never since fallen to its lot. A death-blow was given in 845 to its further progress as a living faith, after which it dragged out an unprofitable existence, as we have already seen, until the fourteenth century, when it disappeared altogether. The events of 845 belong more closely to Buddhism, to which we will now return.

We left Buddhism a flourishing religion at the beginning of the fifth century A.D. It was a period of political disunion, with more than one Emperor in the field, a condition regarded by the Chinese as equivalent to having two suns in the sky. Under the House of Wei, Buddhism was much favoured, and three thousand priests arrived from Turkestan, for whom the Emperor caused over one thousand buildings to be erected in connexion with a large monastery. An official was dispatched to India, in company with a priest, for the purpose of procuring Buddhist books; but although he reached Kandahar, and stayed two years in Udyana, his mission was of little interest compared with another mission, a hundred years later, to which we shall shortly come. The first Emperor of the Liang dynasty (A.D. 502-549) was a devout Buddhist. He lived upon priestly fare, taking only one meal a day; and on two occasions he actually adopted priestly garb, and delivered lectures on the faith. In extension of the Buddhist commandment, "Thou shalt not kill," it was forbidden to weave figures of men, birds, or animals of any kind, in cloth, lest they might some day be cut to pieces; animal sacrifices were also prohibited, and vegetables were used instead.

The next great landmark in the development of Buddhism in China was the arrival of Bôdhidharma, the son of a king in southern India. He had served the twenty-seventh Patriarch for forty years, and at the "transformation" of the latter had been elected to the vacant office. The first Patriarch had been an intimate disciple to whom the Lord Buddha confided, before his entrance into Nirvâna, the secret of the true faith. He may therefore be regarded as the St Peter of Buddhism, the first of a long line of apostles, who handed on the succession from one to another. The fact that the Patriarch was regarded as infallible makes the analogy still more complete; and, in addition, he possessed magical powers. He could fly, and cross water, as we shall see, in a miraculous way. He was the recognized defender of the faith, and he offered an example to all by leading a life of poverty and privation. In the year 520 A.D. Bôdhidharma reached Canton by sea, bringing with him the sacred paten of the Patriarchate, supposed to have been the actual alms-bowl used by Buddha. Summoned to the capital, then at Nanking, he offended the pious Emperor by explaining that real merit lay not in works, but in purity and wisdom duly combined. He therefore retired to Lo-yang in Honan, crossing the swollen Yangtsze on a reed. There he abode for nine years at a temple, sitting in silent contemplation with his face to a wall, and becoming known to the people as the Wall Gazer. He was at length persuaded to give instruction, but about six years later he died. Some one reported having met him after death, crossing a range of mountains *en route* for India, and holding a sandal in his hand; his tomb was therefore opened, and in his coffin was found nothing except the other sandal. His favourite theme was that true religion could not be learnt from books, but that man should seek and find the Buddha in his own heart (see p. 240). He had been the twenty-eighth western Patriarch; he is now reckoned as the first of the Chinese or eastern Patriarchs, in which position he had only five successors. To the people of China he is still familiar as the powerful saint who crossed the Yangtsze upon a reed, a favourite motive of Chinese art.

The second Emperor (A.D. 542-585) of the short-lived Minor Liang dynasty wrote a work upon the mysteries of the *Mahâyâna* and *Hînayâna* schools; and a son of his asked leave to become a Buddhist priest, but repented and wished to cancel his application when he found that his request had been granted. In A.D. 555 an attempt was made by the reigning Emperor of the Northern Ch'i dynasty to fuse Buddhism and Taoism into one religion, and a convocation of priests from both sides was summoned to consider the matter. The Emperor decided in favour of Buddhism, and ordered the Taoists, on pain of death, to shave their heads and become Buddhists. Only four refused, and were executed accordingly.

Such a measure of favour, accorded to an alien religion, was sure, sooner or later, to excite opposition among eminent Confucianists, as well as from the Taoists, who were more concerned with the material profits to be obtained from Court influence. One of the former, named Fu I, a learned scholar who had risen to the post of Historiographer under the first Emperor of the T'ang dynasty, went so far as to present a memorial asking that Buddhism might be altogether abolished. He urged that at any rate priests and nuns should be compelled to marry and bring up families, and not escape from contributing their share to the revenue. The result was that for a time severe restrictions were placed upon the propagation of the faith. One day the Emperor got hold of a Buddhist priest from Turkestan, who could "charm people into unconsciousness and then charm them back to life again," and spoke of his powers to Fu I. "He will not be able to charm me," said the latter confidently; and the priest, when put to the test, failed completely.

In 574 the Emperor took upon himself to arrange an order of precedence for the rival faiths which, at that date, might still be called the Three Religions. Thus, even at the present day, when speaking correctly and not under Buddhist influence, we say Confucianism, Taoism, and Buddhism. Later in his reign the same Emperor prohibited both Taoism and Buddhism, caused the priests of each religion to return to lay life, and their sacred books, images, and temples to be destroyed. Confucianism alone was to stand. Here, then, would seem to be the end of all things in regard to Taoism and Buddhism, but for the fact, familiar to the Chinese people and also to students of Chinese history, that Imperial edicts, unless based upon the will of the people, must always be understood in a Pickwickian sense. Even Chinese Emperors have never been able to prescribe for their subjects in matters of religion, and within five years this drastic prohibition was withdrawn.

A well-known Confucianist poet of the seventh century, named Ch'ên Tzŭ-ang, was offended by the use of idols, which is a feature of Chinese Buddhism but quite foreign to Confucianism. After dwelling on the point that virtue should be practised for its own sake and not with a view to reward in a future life, he goes on to say,

> Now, I have heard the faith by Buddha taught,
> Lauded as pure and free from earthly taint;
> Why then these carved and graven idols, fraught
> With gold and silver, gems, and jade, and paint?
> Fools that ye are! In this ignoble light
> The true faith fades and passes out of sight.

On the other hand, Yao Ch'a, whose name is associated with the history of the Liang dynasty, and who was thought to be the greatest scholar of his day, was a devout Buddhist. At the death of his father, he inherited the title of Duke; upon which he retired to a Buddhist temple, where as a youth he had taken the vows. In his will, he openly professed his belief in the Buddhist faith.

The first Emperor of the T'ang dynasty, who at the instigation of Confucianists had imposed certain restrictions upon Buddhist priests, would also have nothing to do with its Taoist rival. He said, "The Emperor Wu of the Liang dynasty perished through his fondness for Buddhism, and the Emperor Hsüan of the Chow dynasty from trying to teach Taoism; I will take warning and devote myself to Confucianism, which is as necessary to man as wings to a bird or water to a fish." His son and successor was beloved by all priests, Buddhist, Taoist, and even Christian; for it was under his auspices that Nestorian missionaries were allowed to settle at the capital, as we have seen, in the year 636. His own religion was that which Confucius had handed down, and which he expressed on one occasion in the following words: "The people say that the Emperor is supreme and has nothing to fear, but this is not the case with me. Above, I fear the eye of Almighty God; here, I fear the eyes of my officials. I am in constant anxiety, lest on the one hand I disobey the will of God, or on the other lest I disappoint the hopes of my subjects." His Empress shared these views. During her last illness she was urged to turn her thoughts towards Taoism or Buddhism. "These two religions," she replied, "are heretical systems, gnawing at the vitals of the State and distressing the people. The Emperor does not practise them; how then should I, a woman, do this?"

Meanwhile, the Buddhist pilgrim, Hsüan Tsang, was on his famous journey to India, undertaken, like that of Fa Hsien two hundred years before, in order to collect books and images as a help towards the further dissemination of his religion. Born in the year 602, he was educated as a Confucianist; but at the age of twenty, following the lead of an elder brother, he was ordained priest, and in 629 he secretly set out alone on his great adventure. In 645 he returned, and was received with public honours by the Emperor, the Court, and the general public. He brought with him six hundred and fifty-seven Buddhist works, besides many images and pictures, and one hundred and fifty relics. He spent the rest of his life in translating these books, with the help of several learned priests appointed by the Emperor, to whom he submitted, on its completion, the narrative of his travels, known under the title of "A Record of Western Countries."

During the rest of the seventh and the whole of the eighth centuries, the story is the usual one of struggles for Court favour and supremacy between the rival religions, from which even Confucianism did not altogether escape, although invested with an extraordinary prestige which seemed to raise it above the level of all other teachings. We read of both Buddhist and Taoist priests appointed to high office, of an Emperor who saw Lao Tzǔ in a vision, and other similar incidents. In 751 a eunuch was sent as envoy to the king of Kapisa, and among his suite was a youthful civilian, who fell ill and was unable to return to China. As soon as his health began to improve, this young man determined to dedicate his life to Buddha; and he subsequently took the vows, receiving the religious name of Dharmadâtu. He then spent no fewer than forty years wandering through the countries of Central Asia and India, learning Sanskrit and collecting books and relics. At length he returned to China, by land as he had gone, to find, as he said, the trees at his parents' grave already grown to maturity; and he passed the rest of his life translating the *sûtras* he had brought back with him, and advancing the cause of the religion he had so romantically adopted.

In 757 there were several hundred Buddhist priests employed in the palace to conduct religious services; in 765 the Emperor, taking with him two cartloads of the Buddhist Scriptures, proceeded to deposit them in a monastery and to expound their contents. In 768 the Emperor visited a large Buddhist temple which had been built for the repose of his deceased mother, and appointed one thousand priests and nuns, also defraying the expense of annual masses for her soul. In 810 things came to such a pitch that the Emperor received into the palace with great honour a bone of Buddha, which had been originally brought from India and placed in a monastery, where it was exhibited to the populace once in thirty years, and was supposed to have a beneficial influence upon the crops. The relic was kept for three days in the palace, and then passed round to various Buddhist monasteries, where it was on exhibition. This outrage upon conventions was too much for the Confucianists of the day, as represented by Han Wên-kung, one of the greatest in the long roll-call of China's great men. He had already been degraded sixteen years before, for an offensive memorial on the subject of tax-collection; but now, at the age of fifty-one and full of honours, he rose again to the occasion, and presented another more offensive still. He begins by pointing out that Buddhism is a religion of barbarians, of late introduction into China, and quite unknown to the ancients. He shows that the monarchs of old enjoyed long lives without Buddhism, and that not only the Emperors but also the dynasties of Buddhistic tendencies had always been short-lived; and he further enlarges upon the bad example which will be set by the Emperor to an ignorant people. The memorial ends thus: "Buddha was a barbarian. His language was not the language of China. His clothes were of an alien cut. He did not teach the maxims of our ancient rulers, nor conform to the customs which they had handed down. He did not appreciate the bond between prince and subject, the tie between father and son. Supposing, indeed, that this

Buddha had come to our capital in the flesh, under an appointment from his own State, then your Majesty might have received him with a few words of admonition, bestowing on him a banquet and a suit of clothes, previous to sending him out of the country with an escort of soldiers, and thereby have avoided any dangerous influence on the minds of the people. But what are the facts? The bone of a man long since dead and decomposed, is admitted, forsooth, within the precincts of the Imperial palace Did not Confucius say, 'Revere spiritual beings, while maintaining always a due reserve'? When the princes of old paid visits of condolence to one another, it was customary for them to send on a magician in advance, with a peach-wand in his hand, whereby to expel all noxious bewitchments previous to the arrival of his master. Yet now your Majesty is about to introduce, without cause, a disgusting object, personally taking part in the proceedings without the intervention either of the magician or of his peach-wand. Of the officials, not one has raised his voice against it; of the censors, not one has pointed out the enormity of such an act. Therefore your servant, overwhelmed with shame at such slackness, now implores your Majesty that the bone may be handed over for destruction by fire or water, whereby the root of this great evil may be exterminated for all time, and the people know how much the wisdom of your Majesty surpasses that of ordinary men. The glory of such a deed will be beyond all praise. And should the Lord Buddha have power to avenge this insult by the infliction of some misfortune, then let the vials of his wrath be poured out upon the person of your servant, who now calls God to witness that he will not repent him of his oath. In all gratitude and sincerity, and with fear and trembling, your servant now humbly presents this memorial for your Majesty's benign consideration." The phrase "with fear and trembling" was only a formal one to Han Wên-kung. He risked death in the cause of Confucianism, and would certainly have been executed, but for the powerful intercession of friends; as it was he was banished, temporarily as it turned out, to what were then the wilds of Kuangtung.

There is another side, so to speak, to this picture. For just as, in the west, religious feeling is a matter of temperament, and has nothing to do whatever with intellect, so in China many whose intellects, eminently powerful, have been trained on strictly Confucian lines, nevertheless turn, by what is to them a natural instinct, towards the hope of something—anything rather than nothing—beyond the promises—if such there be—held out by the simple teachings of Confucianism. Thus, we have the spectacle of Liu Tsung-yüan, a celebrated poet and essayist, a contemporary and intimate friend of Han Wên-kung, like whom he was banished on political grounds to a distant post, pleading the cause of the religion which the latter so deeply detested. His breadth of intelligence allowed him to tolerate Buddhism, in direct opposition to the utterances of Han Wên-kung, who perceived in its growing influence a menace to Confucianism and to the State. Here are his thoughts on the subject: "My learned and esteemed friend, Han, has often reproached my sympathy with Buddhism and the intercourse I hold with its priests. In point of fact, there is much in Buddhism which could not well be denounced; to wit, all those tenets which are based on principles common to our own sacred books. And it is precisely to these essentials, at once in perfect harmony with human nature and the teachings of Confucius, that I give in my adhesion. My friend says that Buddha was a barbarian. But if this argument is good for anything, we might find ourselves embracing a criminal who happened to be a fellow-countryman, while neglecting a saint whose misfortune it was to be a foreigner. My friend also objects to the Buddhist commandments. He objects to the bald pates of the priests, their dark robes, their renunciation of domestic ties, their idleness, and life generally at the expense of others. So do I; but he misses the kernel while railing at the husk. He sees the lode, but not the ore; I see both, which accounts for my partiality to the faith. Besides, intercourse with men of this religion does not necessarily imply conversion. Even if it did, Buddhism admits no envious rivalry for place or power. The majority of its adherents love only to lead a simple life of contemplation amid the charms of hill and stream. And when I bend my gaze towards the hurry-scurry of the age, in its daily race for the seals and tassels of office, I ask myself if I am to reject those in order to take my place among these."

This writer was the author of answers to the famous questions, already described, which had been addressed to God by the poet Ch'ü P'ing, *al.* Ch'ü Yüan, of the fourth century B.C.; but these answers have never been regarded as worthy of his reputation, being random statements rather than reasoned replies. That the Confucian concept of a Supreme Being was often present to his mind and seriously occupied his thoughts, we can discover from the following short essay, based upon the familiar theory of design. "Over the western hills the road trends away towards the north, and on the further side of the pass, separates into two. The westerly branch leads to nowhere in particular; but if you follow the other, which takes a north-easterly turn, for about a quarter of a mile, you will find that the path ends abruptly, while the stream forks to enclose a steep pile of boulders. On the summit of this pile there is what appears to be an elegantly built look-out tower; below, as it were a battlemented wall, pierced by a city gate, through which one gazes into darkness. A stone thrown in here, falls with a splash suggestive of water; and the reverberations of this sound are audible for some time. There is a way round from behind up to the top, whence nothing is to be seen far and wide except groves of fine straight trees, which, strange to say, are grouped symmetrically, as if by an artist's hand. Now, I have always had my doubts about the existence of a God; but this scene made me think that He really must exist. At the same time, however, I began to wonder why He did not place it at some worthy centre of civilization, rather than in this out-of-the-way barbarous region, where for centuries there has been no one to enjoy its beauty. And so, on the other hand, such waste of labour and incongruity of position disposed me to think that there could be no God after all. One friend suggested that the spot was designedly chosen in order to gratify virtuous men who (like the writer) might be banished thither in disgrace. Another argued that it was simply a question of the nature of the locality; but I do not accept either explanation."

Han Wên-kung entertained no such doubts as these; and when his friend died at the early age of forty-six, in the brief funeral farewell which he burnt at the grave, he spoke of him as one "released in mid-career, by God, from earthly bonds."

The son and successor of the Emperor who received Buddha's bone, said to have been a finger-bone, with such honour, turned his attention rather to Taoism. This shortened his reign; for he died, only four years after his accession, from an over-dose of the elixir of immortality. The check that Buddhism had received from the energetic action of Han Wên-kung, and the restrictive measures he adopted on being recalled from banishment to high office, offered a better chance to the Taoists than they had enjoyed for some time. Han Wên-kung himself had not the same dread of Taoism as he had of the foreign religion; partly, no doubt, because he saw that Taoism, with its borrowed plumes, was purely a money-grinding concern, and had a much weaker hold, as a religion, over the popular imagination; while as a philosophic cult, it was only for the educated student, and was likely to do little harm. In one of his finest essays, "On the True Faith of a Confucianist," he does indeed attack both religions in terms of equal severity. He shows how, under the Han dynasty, the teachings of Lao Tzǔ and Buddha and several heterodox philosophers disturbed men's minds to such an extent that the spirit of Confucianism began to die out, and a general state of apathy to prevail. It may not be amiss to quote here a passage from this uncompromising essay: "The followers of Lao Tzŭ say, 'Confucius was a disciple of *our* Master.' The followers of Buddha say, 'Confucius was a disciple of our Master.' And the followers of Confucius, by dint of hearing this so often, have at length fallen so low as themselves to indulge in such random talk, saying, 'Our Master also respected Lao Tzŭ and Buddha.' Not only have they uttered this with their tongues, but they have written it down in books; and now, if a man would cultivate morality, from whom should he seek instruction? Great is the straining of mankind after the supernatural! Great is their neglect of fundamentals in this yearning for the supernatural alone."

Han Wên-kung proceeds to draw a picture of his countrymen as seen under the rule of their ancient kings, concluding as follows: "Happy in their lives, they were remembered after death. Their sacrifices were grateful to Almighty God, and the spirits of the departed rejoiced in the honours of ancestral worship. Let us then insist that the followers of Lao Tzŭ and Buddha behave like ordinary mortals. Let us burn their books. Let us turn their temples into dwelling-houses." Yet the writer of these words could himself confess to a friendly intimacy with a Taoist priest. Describing in another of his essays a beautiful country scene, he says, "One would naturally conclude that such a spot must be the birthplace of genius, the home of loyal and honourable and virtuous men. But I never saw any; for the people round about are sunk in superstition, in the worship of Lao Tzŭ and of Buddha. However, there is my friend Liao, a priest of the religion of *Tao*. He is a native of these parts, and a man of infinite learning and goodness of heart. How can I class him among those who grovel in superstitious depths? I asked him concerning this strange paradox, but he would not discuss the question, and I must await a more favourable opportunity."

Han Wên-kung died twenty years before the great Taoist revival, which culminated, in the year 845, in an attack upon Buddhism, of greater severity than any to which that faith had hitherto been subjected. We can form some estimate of the attack from the Imperial proclamation which was then issued; the only wonder is that Buddhism should have survived at all. "We have heard," says the Emperor, "that in the early ages the name of Buddha was unknown. It was from the time of the Hans (B.C. 206–A.D. 220) that his images and doctrines became familiar institutions in the land. The strength of man was lavished over his shrines; the wealth of man was diverted to their costly adornment with gold and jewels. Unsurpassed was the injury to public morals; unsurpassed the injury to the welfare of the people! A man who does not work suffers bitter consequences in cold and hunger. But these priests and priestesses of Buddha consume food and raiment without contributing to the production of either. Their handsome temples reach up to the clouds and vie with the palaces of kings. The vice and the corruption of the dynasties which followed upon the introduction of Buddhism, can be attributed to no other source. The founders of my House put down disorder by might, and then proceeded to govern by right. With these two engines of power, they succeeded in establishing their rule. Shall then some paltry creed from the west be allowed to dispute with Us the sovereign power? At the beginning of the present dynasty (A.D. 618), efforts were made to get rid of this pest; but its extermination was not complete, and it became rampant once more. Now, We, having extensively studied the wisdom of the ancients, and guided, moreover, by public opinion, have no hesitation in saying that this evil can be rooted out. Already, more than four thousand six hundred monasteries have been destroyed; and their inmates, to the number of two hundred and sixty-five thousand persons of both sexes, have been compelled to return to the world. Of temples and shrines, more than forty thousand have likewise been demolished; while many thousands of fat acres have been added to the wealth of the people. The work which my predecessors left undone, I have thus been able to accomplish."

Two years later, another Emperor came to the throne, who at once issued orders for all Buddhist temples to be rebuilt; although it was still forbidden to become a priest or nun without proper authorization. His real sympathies, however, were with Taoism, and he went so far as to consult one of the Taoist hierarchy as to the best means of securing eternal life. "Cast aside all desires," answered the priest, who must have been a Taoist in the older and loftier sense of the word; "prize virtue; and the rest will follow as a matter of course." This unsatisfactory advice was promptly rejected, and not long afterwards the Emperor poisoned himself, as usual, with the elixir of immortality. The next Emperor, who began his reign in the year 860, turned the tables once more in favour of Buddhism, which he patronized largely, to the detriment of public affairs. Once more the palace was overrun by priests and nuns, and the Emperor himself joined in chanting the liturgies. Officials were dispatched to receive another relic of Buddha, and gratuitous vegetarian meals were provided for a large number of persons. The State, indeed, had become a mere shuttlecock, to be bandied backwards and forwards between the supporters of the two rival religions. Meanwhile, the great T'ang dynasty, after nearly three hundred years of glory, was rapidly coming to an ignoble end. It collapsed altogether in 905; after which, for some fifty years, the country was hardly in a condition favourable to the development of either Buddhist or Taoist doctrines.

So far no mention has been made of Mahometanism, which also first reached China during the T'ang dynasty, and is still professed by considerable numbers in certain parts of the Chinese empire. Very little indeed is really known, with anything like historical certainty, of the early centuries of this religion. No monument has yet been discovered, similar to the Nestorian tablet, from which the desired information might be gleaned; nor does Chinese official history afford the slightest clue to the establishment of a faith which even now has by no means lost its grip. Various accounts of this important incident have been provided in purely Mahometan-Chinese literature dating from the seventeenth century and onwards, some of which must be taken with reservations. For instance, a Mahometan mission, led by Wahb-Abi-Kabcha, a maternal uncle to the Prophet, is said to have reached Canton by sea in A.D. 628. The mission travelled overland to Ch'ang-an, the capital, and was well received by the Emperor, who graciously accepted as tribute the presents offered.

The first mosque was built at Canton, where, after several restorations, it may still be seen. The minaret, known as the Bare Pagoda, to distinguish it from a much more ornamental Buddhist pagoda near by, dates back to 850. There must at that time have been a considerable number of Mahometans in Canton, though not so many as might be supposed if reliance could be placed on the figures given in reference to a massacre which took place in 879. The fact is that most of these Mahometans went to China simply as traders; they did not intend to settle permanently in the country, and when business permitted, they returned to their old haunts. About two thousand Mussulman families are still to be found at Canton, and a similar number at Foochow; descendants, perhaps, of the old seaborne contingents which began to arrive in the seventh and eighth centuries. These remnants have nothing to do with the stock from which came the comparatively large Mussulman communities now living and practising their religion in the provinces of Ssŭch'uan, Yunnan, and Kansuh. The origin of the latter was as follows. In A.D. 756 the Khalifa Abu Giafar sent a small army of three thousand Arab soldiers to aid in putting down a rebellion. These soldiers had permission to settle in China, where they married native wives; from which it is obvious that the present Mahometan population, their descendants, and also those Mahometan communities at Canton and Foochow, where the same conditions prevailed, are practically of pure Chinese blood. In 798 the Khalifa Harun-al-Raschid dispatched a mission to China, and there had been one or two less important missions in the seventh and eighth centuries; but from 879, the date of the Canton massacre, for more than three centuries to follow, we hear nothing of Mahometans and their religion. They were not mentioned in the edict of 845, which proved such a blow to Buddhism and Nestorian Christianity; perhaps because they were less obtrusive in the propagation of their religion, a policy aided by the absence of anything like a commercial spirit in religious matters. [1]

In 960 China was once again a united empire under the House of Sung. The House of T'ang, with its three hundred years of rule (618-906), stands out as an epoch of brilliant poets and painters, the like of whom have not since been seen. It was also an age of highly-strung religious sentiment, which degenerated into gross superstition. The Sung dynasty, the duration of which was also about three hundred years, is distinguished rather for its solid scholarship, its philosophy, and its scepticism, though poets and painters of the first rank were not wanting, and there were also periods when superstition was rife. The founder of the line, an extraordinarily able man, turned for his hopes of successful government to Confucianism. He caused the Confucian temples to be put into repair, and portraits of the Master and his disciples to be painted. He himself wrote a panegyric on Confucius and the favourite disciple Yen Hui, panegyrics on the other disciples being provided by scholars of the day. His brother, who succeeded him, failed to preserve the Confucian tradition, and showed signs of a tendency to Buddhism; while the third Emperor, son of the last, affected Taoism, and became an easy prey to impostors. Written revelations began to be received from God, and these, by order of the Emperor, were lodged in special temples. In the year 1008 a high official, Wang Ch'in-jo, produced a letter, written on silk and about twenty feet in length, which he declared had come down from heaven and was addressed by God to the Emperor; and when opened, it was found to contain congratulations, expressed in archaic language, on the just government and prosperity of the country which prevailed. The Court officials, who had been summoned to assist, on

---

[1] *See Recherches sur les Musulmans Chinois*, by Prof. A. Vissière.

their knees, at the reading, now saw a purple cloud, shaped like a dragon and a phœnix, descend and hang over the palace buildings. This roused the anger of another high official and scholar of the day. "I have heard," he cried, quoting Confucius, "that God does not even speak; how then should He write a letter?" We must consider this episode in chastened silence, remembering that our own old chroniclers of the twelfth century, Roger of Hoveden and Roger of Wendover, both mention the receipt of a letter from Christ, on the prevailing neglect of the Sabbath.

The next step on the part of those who thus took advantage of the Emperor's superstitious feelings, was to persuade him to offer, at the summit of Mt. T'ai in Shantung, the sacrifices to God the Father and Earth the Mother, to which allusion has already been made, and for which purpose Wang Ch'in-jo, the fabricator of the letter from God, was appointed Master of the Ceremonies. The Emperor, who with all his faults was a humane ruler, issued a special decree that no exactions were to be levied upon the people along the route to the mountain, and also that carts and horses were to be strictly prevented from doing injury to the crops. From the beginning of the tenth month, during which the pilgrimage was to be performed, the Emperor further forbade the slaughter of any animal throughout the empire, he himself living only on coarse vegetables. Music, too, was prohibited, until the moment when it would be used at the opening of the sacrificial ceremonies. During the ascent of the mountain, in spite of its steepness, the Emperor sometimes walked and sometimes rode in a sedan-chair; those of his suite who were unfit for mountain climbing were pulled and pushed up by lusty soldiers, whose shoes were fitted with iron crampons. All along the tortuous path up to the summit, guards were stationed, two paces apart and connected together by strips of silk; even the trees were swathed in silk. At dangerous points, the Emperor always got out of his sedan-chair and went on foot. On the following morning a throne was arranged for God on the top of the round terrace, where seats were reserved for the two predecessors of the Emperor, the letters received from heaven being also deposited there. The Emperor, duly robed, then mounted the terrace alone, all soldiers, sedan-chair and torch bearers, and others, being sent away to a distance. He proceeded to offer certain jade tablets on which had been inscribed addresses, rather than prayers, as may be seen from this specimen. "I, Thy subject, and son by heredity, venture to make a declaration to the Lord God of Heaven. I have inherited Thy glorious mandate to make manifest my services to heaven above. To my uncle, the first of our line, the throne was quietly yielded; my father, the second Emperor, by his zeal and diligence brought about a state of good government. He purified the world; he caused all axle-trees and written characters to be uniform throughout the empire; but he firmly refused to ascend this mountain and make his report, wishing to collect still further blessings. Divine authority has conferred this honour upon me; auspicious omens have come from every side; foreign nations all cherish us; many years of abundance have responded to our desires; and I now reverently perform these sacrifices, in the hope of securing happiness for the black-haired masses. I have carefully selected jade, silk, the proper victims, vessels filled with millet, etc., in order by means of this burnt offering to testify to my perfect sincerity. O my deceased uncle, the first Emperor, and my deceased father, the second Emperor, who sit by God's side and are associated in His power, deign to accept these sacrifices!"

On his way home from Mt. T'ai, the Emperor passed the birthplace of Confucius and conferred upon the sage the title of "King"; six years afterwards he visited a temple he had built in honour of Lao Tzŭ, and invested the Taoist philosopher with the title of "Emperor." Two years later he convened a huge assembly of Taoist and Buddhist priests to consider why it was that the planet Venus had appeared in the daytime, and to avert by prayer any evil consequences therefrom.

These kaleidoscopic phases of religious feeling on the part of Emperors were reflected in the lives of the people, and the natural result was an instability of national faith in any given direction. The spirit of Confucianism, soon to obtain a permanent triumph, was kept alive among the educated. As an example, we may take the life of Chao Pien, an official of the eleventh century, celebrated for his benevolence and integrity, two virtues placed by Confucius in the very front rank. His fearless outspokenness as Censor gained for him the sobriquet of the Censor with the Iron Face; his wise administration in times of great distress caused him to be regarded as the saviour of the people. But it is not on these accounts that he is mentioned here. It is because every night, on retiring, he was accustomed to put on his official robes, and with offerings and incense to submit to Almighty God the events of the day. That God was the God of ancient China, the God of the Odes, now about to disappear, almost altogether, in the coming apotheosis of the greatest of all His prophets.

A.D. 1000-1915

THE eleventh century was not favourable to the growth either of Buddhism or of Taoism. In 1033 the Emperor, who at the age of twenty had just taken over the reins of government, gave orders to stop building or repairing any more temples; and from this date it is noticeable that the two religions no longer wielded quite the same influence at Court as under the T'ang dynasty, neither were the people so often confused by those sudden transitions from one faith to the other. A reason for this may be found in the number of remarkable men, ardent supporters of Confucianism, who were the product of this age. There was Ch'êng Hao, a profound scholar, who soon made his reputation as an official by the suppression of a stone image of Buddha, which had been acquired by some Buddhist monastery, and which was said to emit bright rays, once a year, from its head. Large crowds of men and women were attracted to witness the miracle, and disorderly scenes ensued. Ch'êng Hao invited the abbot to forward the image to his official residence, alleging that he had been unable to inspect it in public, the result being that the spiritual manifestation was no longer continued.

There was Wang An-shih, the socialist reformer, who based his economic innovations upon new interpretations of the Confucian Canon, and whose tablet was placed in the Confucian temple, only to be removed a hundred and forty years later, when it was discovered that he had neither written nor done anything to advance the cause for which the temple had been established. As before stated, the Chinese, like other nations, have often been too hasty in their canonizations; but, unlike many other nations who preserve memorials of persons scarcely entitled to national remembrance, the Chinese, sooner or later, admit their mistake, and cancel the injudiciously granted diploma. One striking example belongs to this very time. A statesman, poet, and essayist, whose name, Su Tung-p'o, is still a household word, and whose writings fascinate all students, died in the year 1101. In 1235, one hundred and thirty-four years afterwards, his tablet was placed in the Confucian temple. It was wrongly so placed; for although his writings may be styled imperishable, they in no way help to demonstrate the truth and value of Confucianism. Yet that tablet remained in its place of honour for over six hundred years, to be removed only so recently as 1845.

His views with regard to the old Confucian concept of God may be gathered from a well-known short essay, entitled "The Arbour to Joyful Rain." On his appointment as Governor at a new post, he put his garden in order and built himself a kiosque near some running water, "intending," as he says, "to use it as a refuge from the business of life. In that very year," he continues, "it rained wheat (see p. 55); and the soothsayers predicted in consequence that the ensuing year would be most prosperous. However, for a whole month no rain fell, and the people became alarmed at the prospect. Then rain fell at intervals, but not in sufficient quantities. At length it poured incessantly for three days. Thereupon, great congratulations were exchanged between officials; tradesmen and traders sang songs of glee in the market-place, while farmers wished each other joy across the furrowed fields. The sorrowful were gladdened; the sick were made whole. And precisely at that moment my kiosque was completed. So I spread a feast there, and invited a number of guests, of whom I inquired, What would have happened if the rain had held off five days longer? There would have been no wheat, was the answer. And what if it had been ten days? I continued; to which they replied that then there would have been no crops at all. And had there been neither harvest of wheat nor of any other grain, said I, a famine must inevitably have ensued. The law courts would have overflowed with litigation. Brigandage and robbery would have been rife. And you and I would have missed the pleasant meeting of to-day beneath this kiosque. But God did not leave the people to perish. Drought has been followed by rain, and to rain it is due that we are enjoying ourselves here now. Shall we then let its remembrance fade away? I think not; and therefore I have called this kiosque 'The Arbour to Joyful Rain,' and I have added to the record the following verses:

> Should the sky rain pearls,
> The cold cannot wear them as clothes;
> Should the sky rain jade,
> The hungry cannot use it as food.
> It has rained without cease for three days;
> Whose was the influence at work?
> If you say it was that of your Governor,
> The Governor himself refers it to the Emperor;
> But the Emperor says, No, it was God,
> And God says, No, it was Nature.
> And as Nature lies beyond the ken of man,
> I dedicate this kiosque to Rain."

In a very beautiful elegy on Han Wên-kung (p. 212) there are several lines which seem to show that Su Tung-p'o's belief in a personal God was a very lively and real one. He claims, in highly poetical language, that Han Wên-kung came straight from heaven at birth, almost "trailing clouds of glory."

> The wind bore him delicately from the throne of God.

Then, after sketching his brilliant career, not forgetting his attack upon Buddhism—

> He cursed Buddha; he offended his prince,

the poet goes on to say,

> But above in heaven, there was no music, and God was sad,
> And summoned him to his place beside the throne.

Su Tung-p'o died in the first year of the twelfth century, which opened with a brief recrudescence of Taoism, and ultimately proved fatal to the continued existence of the old religious belief in a personal God, which, obscured intermittently by Buddhism and Taoism, had still up to this date exercised considerable sway over the minds of the Chinese people. Already, during the eleventh century, a school of metaphysicians had arisen, the leaders of which sought for some more precise solution of the riddle of the universe than had so far been deduced from the Confucian Canon; but it was reserved for the following century to produce, A.D. 1130, one who carried out the movement to such purpose that his name has ever since stood easily first among Chinese philosophers of that or of any other age. A few words are necessary to introduce this very remarkable man.

Chu Fu Tzŭ, as he is popularly called, distinguished himself as a boy by his aptitude for learning, and took the highest degree when only nineteen years of age. In accordance with the usual routine, he was drafted into government employ, and showed considerable success as an administrator. He had previously been suspected of a strong leaning towards Buddhism—some say that he actually became a Buddhist priest; however, by the year 1154, under the guidance of an able teacher, he had seen the error of his ways, and had given himself up to the study of orthodox doctrines. This study he continued all through his career, especially during intervals of forced retirement, until he was finally driven from office by accusations of sedition, magic, breaches of loyalty and of filial piety, with other similarly absurd charges. He passed the evening of his days in literary pursuits, soothed by the ministrations of a faithful disciple. At his death, his coffin is said to have taken up a position, suspended in the air, about three feet from the ground; until his son-in-law, falling on his knees beside the bier, reminded the departed spirit of the great principles of which he had been such a brilliant exponent in life,—and the coffin descended gently to the ground. He had been a most voluminous writer of history, philosophy, and poetry; and he had succeeded in placing himself first among all the commentators on the Confucian Canon. He introduced interpretations either wholly or partly at variance with those which had been put forth by the scholars of the Han dynasty and up to that date received as infallible, thereby modifying to a certain extent the prevailing standard of political and ethical values. He achieved this by the simple process of consistency. He refused to interpret words in any given passage in one sense, and the same words, occurring elsewhere, in another sense. Thus, it has been said that "Shao Yung tried to explain the Canon of Changes by a numerical key, and (another philosopher) Ch'êng I by the eternal fitness of things; but Chu Fu Tzŭ alone was able to pierce through the meaning and appropriate the thought of the inspired men who composed it."

Under the hand of Chu Fu Tzŭ, the idea of a personal God, the supreme ruler of the universe, disappeared for ever. That no proof of the existence of such a Being was forthcoming, was quite enough for his materialistic mind; and being unable, like Cardinal Newman, to dispense with logic and to rely solely upon consciousness, he set to work to frame a cosmogony of his own, in which the God of his fathers was degraded to an abstraction. His universe was developed from a state of Nothing, which somehow became consolidated into Unity, the primeval mother-cell, the bipartition of which produced the *Yin* and the *Yang* (p. 4), the female and male principles. The interaction of these gave birth to the five elements—earth, wood, water, fire, and metal—and through them to all objects, terrestrial and celestial alike. He postulated (1) *ch'i*, which appears to be a formative agent, underlying all matter; not actually itself matter, but rather an all-pervading, subtle, imponderable, vivifying fluid which informs all things and makes them what they are; suggestive of, but not identical with, ether. (2) *Li*, a governing agent, which, like *ch'i*, is omnipresent, and determines the relationship of things to the universe and to each other. No two foreign students are at one as to the correct rendering or even the meaning of the terms *ch'i* and *li*; on the other hand, all native scholars seem to reach the same standpoint of interpretation, as gathered, of course, from the writings of Chu Fu Tzŭ. However this may be, it is with the latter term, *li*, the eternal principle of right, which I have ventured to call a governing agent, that Chu Fu Tzŭ identifies *T'ien*, the God of the Odes, who, as we have seen, is there arrayed in terrors and punishes the evil-doers among mankind. It is true that Chu Fu Tzŭ recognizes this difficulty, and sometimes speaks as though the evidence of antiquity was too much for his arguments; but when all is said and done, his antitheistic attitude asserts itself, and leaves the student with a God who is nothing more than what we call abstract right, operating through the laws of nature. Hence the outwardly atheistic attitude of the modern Confucianist, fed upon the teachings of Chu Fu Tzŭ, who, ever since his death in A.D. 1200, has been accepted as the one and only authority upon the interpretation of the Canon.

Another important subject which Chu Fu Tzŭ discussed at length with his disciples and others was the nature of man at birth, with direct reference to the statement and arguments of Mencius, based, as we have seen, upon tradition, that man is born good. In dealing with this question, disposed of by Mencius in a few words, we are led into rambling and sometimes inconsistent speculations as to the identity of nature in man, animals, and plants, Chu Fu Tzŭ being on the side of an absolute uniformity of nature throughout the universe; and also as to the character of the goodness with which man is endowed, its permanence even in the presence of evil, the fact that evil must have been developed coincidently with the recognition of goodness, etc., etc. Chu Fu Tzŭ argued that the goodness of man at his birth was like a clear spring of water, which becomes defiled by mud as it flows down the hillside; in spite of turbidity, the clear water is still there, and will reappear if the mud is allowed to settle. The foreign student, however, will find considerable turbidity, and not a little inconsistency, in these lucubrations, owing perhaps to the elusiveness of the subject as presented in a difficult language, and not to any want of skill on the part of the great Chinese philosopher.

Chu Fu Tzŭ deals with Taoism and Buddhism on not very statesmanlike lines, and his details are often inexact. Having eliminated God, and the supernatural in general, from the Confucian Canon, which was henceforth to be the undisputed guide of the Chinese people, it was not likely that he would regard with satisfaction, or even with indifference, any other doctrines which conflicted, ever so little, with the results of his own labours. From his time onwards, Confucianism certainly occupied a place by itself, beyond reach of cavil or rivalry. Gradually, it came to be understood that religions of all kinds might flourish or might fade, so long as the Confucian teaching was recognized as supreme. This view was emphasized under the Ming dynasty by an ingenious and not provocative rule. Every temple, Buddhist and Taoist, and every mosque throughout the empire, was compelled to exhibit on the altar, or in some equally conspicuous position, a small tablet inscribed with a formula of allegiance to the Emperor, the head of Confucianism, or as we should phrase it, of the established church.

"Taoism," says Chu Fu Tzǔ, "was at first confined to purity of life and to inaction. These were associated with long life and immortality, which by and by became the sole objects of the cult. Nowadays, they have thought it advisable to adopt a system of magical incantations, and chiefly occupy themselves with exorcism and prayers for blessings. Thus, two radical changes have been made. The Taoists have the writings of Lao Tzǔ and Chuang Tzǔ. They neglected these, and the Buddhists stole them for their own purposes; whereupon the Taoists went off and imitated the *sûtras* of Buddhism. This is just as if the scions of some wealthy house should be robbed of all their valuables, and then go off and gather up the old pots and pans belonging to the thieves. Buddhist books are full of what Buddha said, and Taoist books are similarly full of what *Tao* said. Now Buddha was a man, but how does *Tao* manage to talk? This belief, however, has prevailed for eight or nine centuries past. Taoism began with Lao Tzǔ. Its Trinity of the Three Pure Ones is copied from the Trinity of the Three Persons as taught by Buddhism. By their Trinity the Buddhists mean (1) the spiritual body (of Buddha), (2) his joyful body (showing Buddha rewarded for his virtues), and (3) his fleshly body, under which Buddha appears on earth as a man. The modern schools of Buddhism have divided their Trinity under three images which are placed side by side, thus completely missing the true signification (which is Trinity in Unity); and the adherents of Taoism, wishing to imitate the Buddhists in this particular, worship Lao Tzǔ under (another version of) the Three Pure Ones (see p. 174), namely, (1) as the original revered God, (2) the supreme ruler *Tao*, and (3) the supreme ruler Lao Tzǔ (in the flesh). Almighty God (that is, *T'ien*) is ranked below these three, which is nothing short of an outrageous usurpation. Moreover, the first two do not represent the spiritual and joyful bodies of Lao Tzǔ, and the two images set up cannot form a Unity with him; while the introduction of the third is an aggravated copy of the mistake made by the Buddhists. Chuang Tzǔ has told us in plain language of the death of Lao Tzǔ, who must now be a spirit; how then can he usurp the place of Almighty God? The doctrines of Buddha and Lao Tzŭ should be altogether abolished; but if this is not possible, then only the teachings of Lao Tzŭ should be tolerated, all shrines in honour of him, or of his disciples and various magicians, to be placed under the control of the directors of Public Worship."

Considering that Chu Fu Tzŭ himself reduced the God of the Confucian Canon to an abstraction, it is curious to see how solicitous he is that the Supreme Being shall not be displaced by the members of the Taoist Trinity. And so it has always been with the most rigid Confucianists; they openly accept Chu Fu Tzŭ's definition of God, but at the back of their minds there generally remains a bias in favour of a more personal Deity. It does not come to every man to reach such intimate apperception of the Divine, as to Shao Yung, the philosopher of the eleventh century, whose attempt to explain the Canon of Changes by numbers has already been noted. Remembering that Christ said (Luke xvii. 20, 21), "The kingdom of God cometh not with observation: neither shall they say, Lo here! or Lo there! for, behold, the kingdom of God is within you," the following stanza by Shao Yung has a veritable ring of inspiration:

> The heavens are still: no sound.
> Where then shall God be found?
> Seek not in distant skies;
> In man's own heart He lies.

It is probable that Chu Fu Tzŭ was familiar with the above verse when he formulated his dogma that God is the eternal principle of right. What had been the popular view up to the time of Chu Fu Tzŭ is exhibited in a stanza by Yang I, a precocious boy, also of the eleventh century. On being taken to the top of a pagoda, as is often done in cases of illness, he uttered the following impromptu:

> Upon this tall pagoda's peak
> My hands almost the stars enclose;
> I dare not raise my voice to speak,
> For fear of startling God's repose.

Chu Fu Tzŭ's attacks on Buddhism are very extensive, and although restrained in language, are decidedly searching, especially where he shows that the Buddhists have appropriated so much from the old Taoist philosophers. With one more quotation we will leave this encyclopædic scholar, who found Confucianism a religion, and left it, but for a vital spark, a mere system of ethics. "The aim and object of the Taoists is to preserve free from injury the physical body. The Buddhists, on the other hand, consider the physical body as of no account, but say that there is a something else, quite distinct from the body, which does not come into being at birth, and is not extinguished at death. The fact is that with the consolidation of (lei (the vital fluid) we have the phenomenon of life; with its dispersion we have the phenomenon of death: and all we can do is to fall in with this. Buddhists and Taoists are both equally in fault."

Chu Fu Tzŭ died in the year 1200. In 1163 a number of Persian Jews, under the superintendence of a Rabbi, had found their way into China and had built a synagogue at K'ai-fêng Fu, in Honan. Their simple monotheism was not of the kind to attract much public attention, especially as they adopted the familiar *T'ien* as their equivalent for God; and they seem to have passed almost unnoticed into the general life of the people. It was not until the beginning of the seventeenth century that the presence of Jews in China became known to the western world, when speculation was soon rife as to their identity with the lost tribes of Israel. The story of an earlier arrival of Jews, shortly after the Babylonish captivity, has no foundation in fact.

Ricci, the learned Jesuit missionary, to be mentioned again, then stationed at Peking, one day received a visit from a Chinese official, who claimed to be a co-religionist. It was discovered in conversation that this statement was not substantially exact; however, the report given by this man of a Jewish colony in K'ai-fêng Fu, from which place he had just arrived, induced Ricci to dispatch one of his native Christians thither, to find out how far the story was true. Ricci's messenger brought back several portions of the Pentateuch in Hebrew, but described the Jewish community as very few in number and in the lowest depths of poverty. Several of the Catholic missionaries subsequently visited K'ai-fêng Fu; the account given by the native Christian was verified, and further information collected.

Judaism, which was originally known as the religion of *T'ien chu*, that is, of India, the term India being loosely held to include Persia, came to be called the religion of *T'iao chin*, removing the sinew, in reference to the Jewish preparation of meat, which is thus made *kosher*, or fit for food. It is probable that the change of name was made in order to keep clear of any association with Roman Catholicism, which was also the *T'ien chu* religion, the latter, differently written, being the term adopted by the Catholics as their rendering of God.

In 1850 an important expedition was organized by Protestant missionaries and others. Two native Christians were sent to K'ai-fêng Fu, and by their efforts the question of "Jews in China" was satisfactorily answered once and for all. Besides bringing back portions of the Old Testament in an antique Hebrew form, with vowel points, they had secured copies of certain inscriptions on stone tablets, one of which is of the very highest interest, and achieves for our knowledge of Judaism a result similar to that which was achieved for Christianity by the discovery of the Nestorian tablet. The Jewish stone is dated 1489, and was set up to record the rebuilding of the synagogue on the spot where a synagogue had stood since the first arrival of the Jews in 1163. The inscription opens with a eulogy of Abraham, the Patriarch who founded the religion of Israel, and who was the nineteenth descendant in direct line from Adam. Here the writer, presumably thinking that the name "Adam" would have no meaning for Chinese ears, identifies him with P'an Ku, the Chinese "first man," already mentioned (p. 176) as a member of the Taoist Trinity under one of its varying forms. Altogether there is the same tendency, as in the case of the Manichæans and Nestorians, to work into the new faith as many as possible of the old familiar elements of Chinese belief. For instance, the spiritual regeneration of Abraham is thus described: "Reflecting upon the ethereal purity of God on high, the most adorable, without peer, that Divine Power who does not speak, and yet causes the four seasons to revolve and all things to be produced (these very words were spoken by Confucius); gazing upon birth in spring, upon growth in summer, upon harvest in autumn, and storage in winter; upon creatures that fly, and creatures that swim, upon animals that move, and vegetation that stands still;—how these all flourish and decay, how they bloom and fade, how naturally they grow, undergo change, and take on form or colour—(reflecting and gazing) the Patriarch awakened, as it were from sleep, to the apprehension of this profound mystery. Seeking the true faith, he glorified the one God, serving Him with his whole heart, and revering Him alone; and thus he established our religion, which has endured to the present day."

Moses is next introduced, as one who "by his piety touched the heart of God, and the Bible, in fifty-three books, came into existence of itself." Then, after a warning that "man in his daily life must never for a moment be forgetful of God, but must praise Him in prayer every morning, noon, and evening," we pass into a eulogy of *Tao*, by which is obviously meant the *Tao* of early Taoism, and due recognition of which is adopted as belonging to the worship of the true God. This portion, which has no real significance, is followed by a few historical notes of great value. It is here that the year 1163 is recorded as the date of the first arrival of Jews in China. We are also told that in 1279 the old synagogue was rebuilt, and that in 1386 the first Emperor of the Ming dynasty, in carrying out his policy of pacification, presented the Jewish community at K'ai-fêng Fu with a piece of ground on which they might live in peace and practise their religion without molestation. At that time, says the tablet, the vestments, ceremonies, and music had been modernized, but the language and movements were still according to the ancient rule. In 1421 permission was given for the synagogue to be repaired, with orders that the Imperial tablet should be set up in the building, as a proof of allegiance in spite of dissimilarity of religion. Several other dates of minor importance are added, and the inscription winds up with a statement that Judaism differs almost imperceptibly from the religion of the literati, with which it is at one in the inculcation of loyalty to the sovereign, respect for ancestors, obedience to parents, and other accepted virtues. It was, indeed, just this fact which told against the success of Judaism. Because of the striking similarity between the God of the Odes and the God of the Old Testament, Judaism attracted but little attention, and has now to all intents and purposes ceased to exist. Further, this religion reached China at a time when the obscuration of a Supreme Being, coupled with the apotheosis of a man, was proceeding at a rapid rate, and which the efforts of a few humble Rabbis would be hardly likely to hinder.

The thirteenth century, which witnessed the final overthrow of the Sung dynasty and the establishment of a Mongol domination under Kublai Khan, is especially associated with the rapid spread of Mahometanism in certain parts of China. With the Mongol armies there was a great influx of Mussulmans, reinforcing the earlier communities which we have already noticed. The numbers of these last may have been recruited by the arrival from time to time of Mahometan traders and others, who settled down in the country; still, it is from the thirteenth century onwards that Mahometans became a large and important religious body in the empire. Like their predecessors of the eighth century, they too married native wives, from which it results that their descendants of to-day may really be said to have no trace of Arab blood in their veins. All the same, they are extraordinarily attached to their religion, and will not touch pork, although surrounded by a pig-eating people. During the past three hundred years there have been several serious rebellions, which have taxed all the energies of the Chinese government and of their best generals; but in normal times the Mahometan, allowed to practise his religion in his own way, is a law-abiding citizen, and indistinguishable from the rest of his fellow-countrymen.

Simultaneously with the spread of Islam, we have to note the arrival of what was then universally recognized to be orthodox Christianity. By the year 1289 there was already, in what is now Peking, a Christian bishop, whose chief aim, for a time, was to get rid of the remaining traces of that hateful schism, Nestorian Christianity. Considerable headway seems to have been made, in spite of the political troubles which began to set in during the first half of the fourteenth century; but from the final overthrow of the Mongols and the accession of the House of Ming, very little was heard, for two centuries to come, of any foreign religion, with the exception of Buddhism, which now and again showed signs of renewed Court favour. One statesman, in 1488, caused the Imperial collection of Taoist literature to be burnt; and altogether the period was favourable to the dominance of Confucianism, which a hundred years later was to be confronted by Roman Catholic Christianity, under the guidance of some of the most able men ever attracted to China from the west.

In 1582 the first two Jesuits landed at Canton; they were followed a year later by Ricci, the most distinguished of all the long line of Catholic fathers who have given their lives for service in China, and said to be the only foreigner whose name has ever been mentioned in the dynastic annals. In addition to a variety of scientific work, the skilled performance of which gained for him the intimate patronage of the Emperor, he succeeded in converting to Christianity Hsü Kuang-ch'i, an eminent scholar who ultimately rose to be a Minister of State. He particularly directed his attention to an attack upon Buddhism, the severity of which attack called forth numerous replies from the better educated of the priesthood, and evoked a controversy in which it was considered that Ricci had the better of his opponents. The question as to the admission of ancestor-worship among Christian rites for native converts did not become acute during Ricci's lifetime; he failed, however, to grasp the true inwardness of the ceremony, and gave his opinion in favour of toleration. Later on, there was division in the Jesuit body on the subject; and the Dominicans and Franciscans, who took the narrower but strictly correct view, laid the matter before the Pope, just at the time when the Ming dynasty was collapsing and the conquering Manchus were taking possession of the empire. Pope Innocent X. decided against the Jesuits, but this decision was reversed by his successor, Alexander VII.; then under the next three Popes, efforts were made to settle the point satisfactorily to both parties.

There raged, at the same time, another bitter controversy as to the correct term for "God" in Chinese. The Jesuits favoured the use of *T'ien* and *Shang Ti*, to both of which the Dominicans and Franciscans strenuously objected, declaring that the former represented nothing more than the material sky, and the latter the spirits of deified Emperors instead of the true God. Their term was *T'ien Chu*, "Lord of the Sky," a term which had been applied, some centuries before Christ, though they did not know it, to the first of Eight Spirits, the other seven of which were the Lords of Earth, War, Darkness, Light, the Moon, the Sun, and the Four Seasons; it was also in use among Buddhists as an equivalent for the Brahmin god, Indra. To stand merely at the head of such a list is hardly in keeping with the majesty of that *T'ien*, the One God of the Odes, who with *Shang Ti* forms a Duality in Unity; and the wonder is that such a term should ever have been adopted. Both the above controversies were submitted by the Jesuits to the Emperor K'ang Hsi, than whom, in point of learning and justice, no more fitting arbiter for the second question could well have been found. He decided (1) that there was nothing in the practice of ancestor-worship which was contrary to the teaching and spirit of Christianity, and (2) that the Chinese word *T'ien* was the right and proper equivalent for God, It is no doubt a sound legal maxim that a litigant shall not be allowed to approbate and reprobate the same instrument; at the risk, however, of violating in a sense this maxim, I am bound to say that I disagree with his Majesty's decision in the first instance, which he was not qualified to give, and agree with it in the second, which is quite another matter.

The upshot of all this squabbling was, first of all, that the Emperor was much affronted when he found that the final Papal decree was against his own views; and secondly, that from this date restrictions were placed upon the freedom of Catholic missionaries, which under later Emperors developed into persecution and attempts to suppress the propaganda altogether. It is generally believed that the Roman Catholic Church had here a real opportunity for the Christianization of China, and lost it. As scholars, the Dominicans and Franciscans could not for a moment compare with the learned Jesuits, and their rejection of *T'ien* as the proper rendering of "God" was a real misfortune; on the other hand, their refusal to let the end justify the means and to admit of rites which they felt were antagonistic to the spirit of their religion, can only redound to their credit.

It remains now to consider what was the religious attitude of the Manchu rulers of China, from the date of their accession to power in 1644 down to the triumph of the republicans in 1912. Beyond a rather vague acquaintance with Buddhism, they do not seem to have entered upon the government of the empire weighted by any serious religious convictions whatever. The second Emperor, K'ang Hsi, was a man of unusual capacity, and held very firmly the Erastian doctrine that religion should be subordinated to politics, coupled with a determined opinion that the two should be kept severely apart. He would have nothing to do with any faith which involved supernatural beliefs; but being wise enough to see that it was absolutely necessary for the masses to have some sort of guidance, he fell back upon Confucianism without God, which, of course, was altogether beyond their reach. The Confucian Canon became more than ever the Bible of educated Chinese, to the authority of which all questions were referred; worship in the various temples of Confucius was earnestly performed, and all forms of classical learning were encouraged. The Emperor himself composed sixteen maxims for everyday life, which were issued in 1691 as a Sacred Edict, the name by which they are now known. It was not a new idea; the first Emperor of the Ming dynasty had issued a similar Edict in six maxims, but the latter never had the same vogue as that of the Emperor K'ang Hsi. Each of these sixteen maxims consisted of seven words. Under the next Emperor, sixteen short essays were prepared by leading scholars of the day, to amplify and illustrate the meaning of the maxims; these essays, however, being in a highly polished book style, were not readily intelligible to the unlettered, and a further effort was made to paraphrase the whole into something approximating to the colloquial language. For it had been ordained that this Edict was to be read publicly on the 1st and 15th of every month in all cities and towns throughout the empire.

We are here concerned with but one of these sixteen maxims, from almost all of which, amplification and paraphrase alike, any suggestion of belief in, or reliance upon, a Supreme Being is markedly absent. We are told, indeed, in the amplification of the first maxim, that "filial piety is the law of God," but this seems to be the sole kind of recognition, unsatisfactory as it is, to be met with in the whole work. There are homely proverbs for the people, such as, "If all your life you yield the path, you will not lose even a hundred yards." The rest is Confucianism, in the modern sense of the term: glorification of Confucius, so far, as an inspired teacher, not yet as a god. The seventh of the sixteen maxims is this: "Get rid of heterodoxy, in order to glorify the true doctrine." In the amplification we read, "When man is born into his place in the universe, he has before him only the five relationships, between sovereign and subject, father and son, husband and wife, brother and brother, and friend and friend. These form a path of duty for all, fools and wise alike, to follow. The inspired men and sages of old would have no prying into mysteries or supernatural practices." Then, after denouncing heterodox books, which eat like worms into the life of the people, the writer continues, "Three forms of doctrine have come down to us from antiquity; for in addition to Confucianism, we have Taoism and Buddhism. The philosopher Chu Fu Tzŭ says, 'The doctrines of Buddhism take no note of anything within the four quarters of the universe, but are concerned only with, the mind. The doctrines of Taoism aim only at preserving physical vitality.' From these impartial words we can see what was the original intention in each case." The amplification goes on to show how, under the cloak of these two religions, abuses have crept in, and evil-disposed persons have combined to perpetrate crimes contrary to public morals. Now comes a more interesting paragraph: "As to the western doctrine which glorifies *T'ien Chu*, the Lord of the Sky (*i.e.* Roman Catholicism), that too is heterodox; but because its priests are thoroughly conversant with mathematics, the government makes use of them,—a point which you soldiers and people should understand." The amplification proceeds to say that all heresies should be dealt with in the same way that robbers, inundations, and fires are dealt with: they should be exterminated.

In the colloquial paraphrase of the above essay, Taoism and Buddhism are denounced in scathing language and held up to ridicule by turns. The graven images, celibacy, fasting, and spiritual promises of the Buddhists, are classed with the exorcism, alchemy, elixir of life, and magical pretensions of the Taoists, as nothing more than ridiculous impostures; and the opportunity is further taken to warn people against the danger of joining secret political societies. Passing on to the strictures upon Christianity, we read, "As to the doctrine of the Lord of the Sky, with its random and unsubstantial talk, that too is not orthodox; but because its priests know all about astronomy and mathematics, the Court makes use of them to construct our calendar. This does not mean to say that their religion is a good one, and you must on no account believe it. The law is very strict in its dealings with these by-path, side-door sects, just as it is with the men and women who practise devil-dances (a form of exorcism), against whom laws and penalties have been enacted." A little further on we have the familiar dogma of the goodness of man at birth: "These heresies and evil teachings seriously injure the bias of the heart; that heart which was given by God to man at his birth, upright and free from wickedness, but which, through greed, has been led astray into wrong paths. For just as the poor want to become some day rich and great, so do the rich and great want to prolong possession of what they have got; they want old age; they want sons and daughters; and what is beyond everything, they want to secure in this life, happiness in the life to come. . . . If you only knew that in everybody's home there are two living Buddhas to be worshipped, what excuse would there be then for going off to worship mountains and for praying for happiness to clay and wooden images? The proverb well says, Stay at home and reverence your parents; why travel afar to burn incense? If you could but grasp the truth, you would know that a bright and happy mind *is* heaven, and that a dark and gloomy mind is hell. Thus, you would have your own God, and would not be deceived by false doctrines."

Printed and published all over the empire, the Sacred Edict proved a serious blow to the immediate spread of Christianity. However, it appears that Roman Catholicism soon rallied from the stroke; and although no longer able to profess the faith quite openly, its priests certainly succeeded in gathering together large numbers of converts over a considerable area. For this statement we have the authority of Lan Lu-chou, one of the most distinguished writers of the eighteenth century. In a paper dated 1732, and entitled "Barbarians in the province of Kuangtung," he makes the following remarks: "The Catholic religion is now spreading over China. In the provinces of Hupeh, Hunan, Honan, Kiangsi, Fuhkien, and Kuangsi, there are very few places which it has not reached. In 1723 the Viceroy of Fuhkien complained that the western foreigners were preaching their religion and tampering with the people, to the great detriment of the localities in question; and he petitioned that the Roman Catholic chapels in the various provinces might be turned into lecture-rooms and schools, and that all western foreigners might be sent to Macao, until an opportunity should present itself for returning them to their own countries. However, the Viceroy, out of mistaken kindness, memorialized the Throne that such of the barbarians as were old or sick, and unwilling to go away, might be permitted to remain, on condition that if they proselytized, or spread their creed, or chanted their sacred books, they were at once to be punished and sent away. The scheme was an excellent one, but where are the results of it? At present, more than ten thousand men have joined the Catholic chapel at Canton, and there is also a department for women, where they have similarly got together about two thousand. This is a great insult to China, and seriously injures our national traditions; 'tis enough to make every man of feeling grind his teeth with rage."

During the opening years of the nineteenth century, Protestant missionaries appeared for the first time upon the scene. For a long period their activities were confined to a very narrow area, in the extreme south, and no attempt was made to follow the Catholic fathers into the interior. Thus, they had little opportunity for proselytizing, and turned their energies to translation. Various immature versions of the Bible, in part or entire, were now produced, of which the less said the better. Even at this late date, it cannot be affirmed with truth that the best translation of the Bible into Chinese reproduces with fidelity the sense and spirit of the original. First of all the "term question" intervened, and made anything like a general harmony impossible; for just as the Catholic orders had quarrelled, so did the Protestant missionaries belonging to different sects quarrel over the selection of a fit and proper rendering for "God," but without the advantage of an infallible Pope to settle the point for them. It was not to be supposed, of course, that the Catholic term would be adopted; and in that there is small cause for regret. The terms ultimately chosen by the opposing sides were *Shang Ti* and Shên (or Shin). The former of these we have already considered, and have ranked it second to *T'ien*; as to *Shên*, it generally represents in Chinese literature those invisible intellectual beings whom we call spirits. It is obvious, therefore, that there must be some difficulty in always restricting the latter term to the One Spirit whom we mean by "God"; indeed, this difficulty was so far appreciated that the word *chên*, "true," was prefixed: *Chên Shên*, "the True Spirit." Here again there is an objection; the word chên is specially associated with Taoism, and is employed in designations of Taoist saints, priests, and wizards, as well as in the Taoist term *Chên Tsai*, the First Cause, which has been adopted by Mahometans as their rendering of "God." In 1847 an attempt was made to produce a satisfactory translation of the Bible by the collaboration of delegates from the various missionary bodies. By 1850 the New Testament was completed; but so strong was the feeling on the subject of terms, that two sets of this translation were printed, with different Chinese renderings for "God" and "Spirit." A further attempt to translate the Old Testament was a failure; at the ninth chapter of Deuteronomy there was a split in the camp, and two of the delegates retired, leaving the work to be completed in 1855 by three of their colleagues who were all, as regards terminology, of the same way of thinking.

The next question that arose was that of style, which has always been such an important feature of Chinese scholarship. The delegates had aimed at a polished classical style, such as would find favour with the literati, and had to some extent succeeded; but the real meaning was often misinterpreted, and style alone failed to recommend a book which, published without a commentary, was largely unintelligible even to educated readers. Other Protestant missionaries, anxious to get the Bible into the hands of the people, now began to make versions, some of which came out as nearly as possible in colloquial, which, of course, would prevent the literati from even condescending to take a look, and did not prove much more intelligible after all. It still remains to produce an accurate translation of the Bible in a good literary style. The translation should not be slavishly literal, for that would obscure the sense; nor the style too low class, for that would give the impression of a low class book. As there is much misconception on the subject of translation into Chinese, a few explanatory words may be allowed. When a foreigner translates a book into Chinese, he does not take his pen and transfer the thought himself; few foreigners are capable of writing even a simple letter by themselves, and certainly no foreigner has yet seen the light who could attempt, unaided, such a work as the Bible, or indeed any portion of it. What the so-called translator does do, is to engage a more or less educated native, and explain to him, as best he can, in colloquial, the text to be rendered into Chinese. If the foreigner is anything of a scholar, and the text offers no special difficulties, he will be able to verify to some extent the translation made; but all the beauties, or artifices, or blemishes in the style, will be the work of his native friend, upon whose ability the literary value of the work depends.

At the present day we find China provided with some half-dozen forms of religious influence. The Manchus made Confucianism their sheet-anchor, and placed their reliance wholly upon its preserving power. From the point of view of the educated, Confucianism is based, as we have seen, upon direct revelation, witnessed in the delivery to man, by supernatural means, of the Eight Diagrams and the arrangement of the numerals 1 to 9, on which was founded a system of divination, followed by the later speculations of the Sung philosophers. In 1908, when their mandate was already exhausted, the Manchus foolishly elevated Confucius to the rank of a god, an honour which the old sage himself would have been the very first to repudiate. Still, during all their tenancy of the empire, the Manchus kept Buddhism (an importation) and Taoism (an imitation) well in hand, and away from political aspirations. The function of these two religions was thus only to satisfy

> . . . the pleasing hope, the fond desire,
> The longing after immortality,

and also to stave off or allay

> . . . the secret dread and inward horror
> Of falling into naught.

Confucianists will not readily avow any faith in either one or the other; at the same time, it is customary for all families to visit Buddhist or Taoist temples—often both, and to employ the priests—also of both, to recite masses for their dead. Exceptional treatment has always been shown to Mahometans, who are regarded as a dangerous element in the State; for instance, because they do not eat pig, they are permitted the use of beef in addition to mutton, although this is contrary to the rule against slaughter of the ploughing ox.

Christianity suffered much from persecution during the nineteenth century. The appearance of Protestantism as an uncompromising opponent of Roman Catholicism, though the same God was worshipped and the same leading doctrines were professed, completely mystified the Chinese, who became more suspicious and more hostile than ever. Roman Catholicism, with its fine cathedrals and ornate ritual, so closely identical in many of its characteristics with Buddhism, has always made a much more effective appeal to the masses; it has also gained, since early days, by presenting a united front instead of being split up, like Protestantism, into many sects, differing from one another in details of doctrine almost as much as the Roman Catholic church differs from any one of them. Lord Kinnaird (*Times*, Dec. 18, 1913) was right when he said, "The weakness of foreign missions has been that we have carried our home divisions into the field where a united foe must be faced. We have deliberately weakened the mission of the church of the living God by our sectarian bias." Time, too, has been on the side of the Catholics, and they have in consequence a very much larger body of converts. On the other hand, Protestantism was less dreaded by the Manchus. Its missionaries interfered less, though often too much, between the authorities and the people who had become converts. They arrogated to themselves no temporal dignities; whereas in 1899 the Catholics succeeded in obtaining from the Chinese government recognition of the Pope as "Emperor of the Faith," and of their bishops as equals in rank with viceroys and governors of provinces.

Speaking now without distinctions of any kind, it may be said without fear of contradiction, that considering the sacrifice, both of blood and of treasure, the growth of Christianity in China has been disappointing to its supporters. Missionaries have had and still have a difficult row to hoe. They found the Chinese people steeped in superstition, but devoid of any real religious sentiment. The Buddhist masses unquestionably believe in a future state—a spiritual reproduction of the present state, from which consciousness is not absent. They have authority for this. A high official named Wang T'an-chih, who flourished in the fourth century A.D., agreed with a friendly Buddhist priest that whoever might die first would return and enlighten the survivor. About a year later, the priest suddenly appeared before Wang and said, "I have lately died. The joys and sorrows of the next world are realities. Hasten to repent, that you may pass among the ranks of the blest." Educated Chinese, however, have no faith in such stories; neither will they accept the early chapters of Genesis, especially now that a distinguished Professor of Divinity (Professor Burkitt) has publicly declared that these chapters contain nothing more than Asiatic folklore. They have difficulties over the divinity of Christ—which is indeed a moot point among European scholars—and over His virgin birth and resurrection, both of which events will be found to have parallels in early Chinese literature. The doctrine of the Trinity, already familiar through Buddhism, naturally forms a severe stumbling-block; the more so to those who discover, or are told, that this important dogma is nowhere mentioned in the Bible, but belongs to a later date.

The Chinese in general are impatient of a weekly day of rest; they do not say grace at meals; they do not understand prayer in our western sense; there is certainly no such thing as "family prayers" from one end of the empire to the other. They will pray at temples, and at fixed dates to the spirits of the dead, but only for benefits to follow. "The maker of images," as the saying goes, "will not pray at all to the gods: he knows what stuff they are made of." When, in 1911, the devoted young medical missionary,

Arthur Jackson, lost his life in fighting the plague in Manchuria, the Viceroy offered, at the memorial service, a prayer which ended thus:

O Spirit of Dr Jackson, we pray you intercede for the twenty million people of Manchuria, and ask the Lord of the Sky to take away this pestilence, so that we may once more lay our heads in peace upon our pillows.

In life you were brave, now you are an exalted spirit. Noble Spirit, who sacrificed your life for us, help us still and look down in kindness upon us all!

All such points, however, fade into insignificance before the three real obstacles to the spread of Christianity in China. These are, first of all, the Confucian dogma that man is born good; secondly, the practice of ancestral worship, which, as has already been shown, is incompatible with Christian doctrine; and thirdly, the rules and practice of filial piety, due directly to the patriarchal system which still obtains in China. It has indeed been seriously urged that the unparalleled continuity of the Chinese nation is a reward for their faithful observance of the fifth commandment. In the face of this deeply implanted sentiment of reverence for parents, it is easy to see what a shock it must give to be told, as in Mark x. 7, 29, 30, that a man shall leave his father and mother and cleave to his wife; also, that if a man leaves his father and mother for Christ's sake and the gospel's, he will receive an hundredfold now in this time, and in the world to come eternal life.

In 1913 the Chinese government made application to Christian churches throughout the world for intercession by prayer on behalf of the young Republic. This request was received with acclamation on all sides, and great hopes were aroused by such an unprecedented act; but

>Hope told a flattering tale,

and in March 1914, the old religious rites performed by the Manchu Emperors almost to their last days, but not by the people, were re-established by the President. It is already announced that on the 23rd December the Head of the State will resume the annual visit to the so-called Temple of Heaven, and, passing alone into the sacred, circular, blue-domed chamber, will report his shortcomings at what is really considered to be an interview with the Most High.[1] The less impressive parts of the ceremony are to consist of genuflexion and burnt offerings; and there is now a proviso that every citizen shall be free to worship in his own family, so as to secure uniformity. Unfortunately, ever since the days of Chu Fu Tzŭ, the idea of a Supreme Ruler of the universe has been much obscured for the people at large by the glorification of Confucius. It is true that the term is still familiar in such sayings as, "God's eye is upon you!" "You can deceive man but not God!" "Do your duty, and leave the rest to God!"— and many others of the kind; still, what the literati have urged for centuries upon the masses is the veneration of Confucius, and not the fear and love of God.

Mr Balfour asserted in his Gifford Lectures that a world without God is a world in which æsthetic and ethical values are greatly diminished, sublimely indifferent to the fact that æsthetic and ethical values have nowhere been so high-pitched as in China and Japan, where for many centuries past God has been almost a negligible quantity. But if it be true in a general sense, as Mr Balfour claims, that a "theistic setting" in human affairs is for the well-being of mankind, then China has now a chance which

---

[1] "On Dec. 23 President Yuan Shih-k'ai, as head of the nation and therefore as direct successor to the Emperor of China, performed the worship of heaven at the Temple of Heaven in accordance with the old-time ceremonial. The old ritual was closely followed, except that there was no burning of a whole bullock, and the kowtow was dispensed with, the President merely bowing to the altar where emperors prostrated themselves. Also, the emperors used to spend the night before the sacrifice in a hall adjoining the altar in meditation and fasting. President Yuan was not absent from his palace for more than an hour all told.

"He wore a gorgeous dress—a kind of "mortar-board" hat tied with purple strings beneath the chin, and adorned with one enormous pearl surrounded by twelve smaller ones arranged in the shape of an ear of rice; a flowing silk robe embroidered with mystic symbols in red and gold; a red silk skirt fringed with gold; and a heavy gold girdle. The attendant officials were hardly less resplendent. All the sacrificial utensils, drums, and gongs of former years were used, arranged with scrupulous attention to due order.

"Accompanied by music, the chanting of supplications, the burning of incense, and many obeisances, the President ascended the marble steps of the great altar, beneath a cloudless sky, and offered, with appropriate ritual, a blue paper inscribed with prayers written in vermilion, a tray containing the blood and hair of a bullock slaughtered the day before, silk, soup, wine, grain, and jade. All except the jade were then burnt in the great brazier adjoining the altar" (*London and China Telegraph*, Feb. 1, 1915).

should not be missed. The Republic is crying out for a State religion. In the words of a famous Chinese poet,

> Stoop, and there it is;
> Seek it not right nor left.

Let the Chinese people be encouraged, by the erection of temples and by forms of prayer, to join in the old unitarian worship of four thousand years ago. Let them transfer to *T'ien*, God, discarding the Duality caused by the later introduction of *Shang Ti*, all those thoughts of reverence and gratitude which have been centred so long upon the human, to the neglect of the divine. Their stirring battle-cry would then be, "There is no God but God, and Confucius is His Prophet!" [1]

---

[1] "Mr Annand (a missionary) reports, with regard to the condition of affairs in the northern provinces, that there has been no evidence of the anti-foreign or anti-Christian feeling which was so prevalent a few years ago, but that there has been a very distinct revival of pagan worship and customs, which in the heyday of the 'reformation' had fallen into disfavour. Confucianism also has been resuscitated, and is now supported strenuously by scholars and those in authority, but its revival is only a phase of the present state of unrest" (*London and China Telegraph*, April 19, 1915).

www.ingramcontent.com/pod-product-compliance
Lightning Source LLC
Chambersburg PA
CBHW051547010526
44118CB00022B/2612